The Essentials of College Teaching

The Essentials of College Teaching

A Guide for New and Adjunct College Instructors

Constance Jones

ROWMAN & LITTLEFIELD
Lanham • Boulder • New York • London

Published by Rowman & Littlefield
An imprint of The Rowman & Littlefield Publishing Group, Inc.
4501 Forbes Boulevard, Suite 200, Lanham, Maryland 20706
www.rowman.com

86-90 Paul Street, London EC2A 4NE

Copyright © 2024 Constance Jones

All rights reserved. No part of this book may be reproduced in any form or by any electronic or mechanical means, including information storage and retrieval systems, without written permission from the publisher, except by a reviewer who may quote passages in a review.

British Library Cataloguing in Publication Information Available

Library of Congress Cataloging-in-Publication Data
978-1-4758-6696-4 (cloth)
978-1-4758-6697-1 (paperback)
978-1-4758-6698-8 (electronic)

This book is dedicated to my teachers. May you have peace, happiness, and health. And to my students. May you have peace, happiness, and health.

Contents

Preface ix
Acknowledgments xi
Chapter 1: The Syllabus 1
Chapter 2: Instructor Presentation 15
Chapter 3: Assessment 31
Chapter 4: Class Management 51
Chapter 5: Tips for the Terrified or Otherwise Unwell 67
Chapter 6: The Syllabus Supplement 77
Chapter 7: Instructor Presentation Supplement 83
Chapter 8: Assessment Supplement 89
Chapter 9: Class Management Supplement 95
Chapter 10: Teaching for the Terrified Supplement 101
Chapter 11: New Instructor Checklist 109
Chapter 12: Instructor Bingo Sheet 113
Index 115
About the Author 117

Preface

Many books focused on the craft of college-level teaching are tailored to tenure-track faculty, who must balance teaching with research and other duties. A number of specialty books also have been published, including texts on balancing teaching and research, tips for teaching online, techniques for teaching certain types of students (e.g., first-generation), and techniques for teaching for certain types of instructors (e.g., African American women). Online teaching resources are available, but locating material involves time-consuming hunting.

This book is intended primarily for the huge number of adjunct college instructors working today, many of whom are hired quickly, and assigned one or more courses with little lead time and less guidance. They don't have the time to dive into a pile of "best practices" academic-type books (*Inside Higher Ed* laughably recommended new instructors read *six* books to prepare for teaching) but would benefit from a quick "down and dirty" guide. This text gives good practical tips for teaching, based on empirical evidence, along with anecdotes to demystify the process of teaching.

I wrote this aiming for a concise, slightly irreverent style. This tone will please many, but is not for everyone (some reviewers have deemed this text "weird" and possibly "snarky"). My hope is that my commitment to the craft of teaching shines through. By learning from this book and implementing best practices, the goal is that instructors will acquire skills that will subsequently benefit students, who will experience a better managed classroom and exposure to improved pedagogy and enhanced learning.

Acknowledgments

Thanks to Lynn Lirette, for talking me through the reason and logic for this book; writing teacher Lydia Yuknavitch, for championing taking risks; other authors, from L. Frank Baum to Anne Lamott, for modeling humor and whimsy; my network of colleagues who have held me in esteem and support; and most of all the students I have had the privilege to teach.

Chapter 1

The Syllabus

The syllabus is frequently described as a course-specific "contract" between the instructor and students. At its best, a syllabus contains answers to frequently asked questions, highlights general policies, gives a sense of the instructor's style, and provides a rough road map for the course as a whole. At its worst, a syllabus reads like a legal contract: indecipherable and therefore so foreign as to provide students a projective opportunity to contemplate their inherent superiority / massive ineptitude / lunch plans.

The syllabus is often the point of first contact between student and instructor. It is also the point of last contact in the event of a grade dispute, with the document carefully scrutinized by chairs, deans, and other administrators. (Remember this as you consider, for example, a hilarious pirate-themed syllabus, complete with doubloons rather than points.

Maybe not.) It is worth concerted effort to make your syllabus as accurate and helpful as possible.

WHAT SHOULD BE INCLUDED IN A SYLLABUS?

Most universities, and often, specific departments, will have required content for syllabi. Typical required content includes:

Term. This may seem obvious, but there exist on this earth multiple syllabi with the incorrect term and year emblazoned upon the top of page 1. Aim to embed your mistakes at least a bit deeper into the syllabus.

Department. Give the complete and accurate name of the department for whom you are working. Occasionally departments change their name. Be sure to keep up-to-date with the department's current fancies.

Course Name. Refrain from cleverly polishing the title of the course. The name, no matter how awkward, should be taken directly from the course catalog.

Units. Similarly, reproduce the number of units listed in the course catalog. Units are essentially a monetary unit to students, and sloppiness in reporting the number of units is a high crime.

Course Time and Location. Provide the time and location of the course classroom. Be sure to spell out the complete name of the building, and also provide the university-selected abbreviation, if such exists. If your course is completely online, indicate this. If your course is a "hybrid" (partially in-person and partially online), be sure to be crystal-clear when you expect to see students in the classroom and the location of the classroom.

Instructor Name. Provide your name, possibly along with your educational degrees. You may want to include a statement indicating how you prefer to be addressed. It is very common for less sophisticated students to address women instructors as Miss or Missus, even if they possess PhDs, in an earnest attempt to be respectful. If you are a woman, it is possible the most important fact you may teach a student the entire term is that women may possess a PhD and can be addressed in the classroom as Doctor or Professor, rather than by their first name or Miss or Missus. If you have a master's degree, it is entirely acceptable to request that students address you as Professor. Younger women instructors, who may have some minor difficulties acquiring authority in the classroom, would do best to not have students casually using their first name.

Instructor Office Location. A number of adjunct instructors may not have offices provided. If you do not have an office on campus, check with the departmental administrative assistant or the chair regarding policies with respect to meeting students outside of class. Email, telephone, or videoconferencing (such as Zoom) may be used for student consultation, if in-person connections are difficult or not allowed (due to social distancing policies, for example).

Instructor Email. List your university-provided email address in the syllabus. Another important meta-message for students is that instructors can have a healthy work/life balance. Use the "schedule" option in email to prevent your emails from being sent after 5 p.m., before 8 a.m., or during weekends or holidays.

Instructor Telephone. Adjunct instructors may not be provided a university telephone number or, if they are, may be given a telephone number to be shared with so many other adjuncts that the telephone may quickly develop a full mailbox or suffer from mysteriously disappearing messages. It is appropriate to request students contact you via email rather than telephone, if that seems most expedient. It is inappropriate to give students your personal home number or cell number. If you do have your own university telephone, remember to actually check for phone messages.

Instructor Office Hours. Check with the university regarding office hour policies. If it is required that instructors hold office hours, yet offices are not provided, ask the departmental administrative assistant or the chair how that is to be accomplished. The library may provide meeting space. Coffee shops or the like are generally inappropriate, given that such issues as accessibility and payment for beverages can swiftly become problematic. Under no circumstances should you meet with students in your home, no matter how charming your etchings. The pandemic era has ushered in virtual office hours, with the instructor setting aside dedicated time each week to email, telephone, or videoconference with students on an as-needed basis.

Course Description. Provide a brief description of the class. Usually this description can be taken directly from the university course catalog. After years of assiduously avoiding plagiarism as students, instructors are sometimes hesitant to literally "cut and paste" boilerplate language into a syllabus. Remember the "contract" essence of the syllabus. You can be guaranteed that university lawyers have vetted any university's boilerplate language, so it is best not to paraphrase. Simply "cut and paste."

Prerequisites for the Course. List these also directly from the course catalog.

Required Course Materials. List required textbooks and other essential materials, including calculators, laboratory clothing or equipment, and iClickers or the like. For each item listed, explicitly check the cost to students. Only require items that are truly necessary.

With respect to textbooks, note that for each course, specific textbooks may be required to be assigned. Or, conversely, textbooks may be discouraged, with a strong push toward the use of free, open-source materials. Inquire about the preferences of the department. If a textbook is encouraged, select one as far in advance of the term as possible, to allow for student accommodations, and keep your eye on price. Students appreciate affordable textbooks. If you do assign a textbook, be sure to explicitly refer to the text and assign readings from the text throughout the term. One compromise is to assign an optional textbook, to give direction for those students who feel they might need supplemental out-of-class guidance.

Course Assignments. Now it's getting serious. Students will look this section over carefully. This is where you communicate to students how they will earn their grade. Detail the number of small quizzes and points per quiz; number of larger examinations and points per examination; ditto for homework, papers, projects, presentations, etc. Policies regarding attendance, participation, and penalties for late work should be included in this section as well (see more details in Chapter 3). In many ways, the course assignments section is like the abstract of a scientific paper. It is often most efficient to write this section after completing your entire syllabus, when you have made a number of important decisions about how you wish to construct your course.

Extra Credit. State your policies for extra credit. A few extra credit activities or assignments reassure students, lessen pressures on you, and reduce the probability of your having to engage in duels with students over two points. Be sure opportunities for extra credit are accessible to all, are connected to academic goals for the course, and comprise a small percentage of points to be earned in the entire course. Despite predictable begging by a few desperate students finding themselves at the cusp of a higher grade at the end of the term, it is unfair and unethical to offer only a subset of students extra credit opportunities.

Grading Policy. Detail precisely how grades will be earned (see more details in Chapter 3). The entire rest of the syllabus may be disregarded by students, but you can be guaranteed they will read this section carefully. For anxiety reduction, on both the part of the instructor and the student, a simple grading scheme (e.g., 90%–100% = A, 80%–89% = B) is often best.

Student Learning Objectives. Student Learning Objectives, or Student Learning Outcomes (SLOs either way), are goals for students' academic accomplishments upon completing a course. Instructors are typically asked to list three to five SLOs in their syllabus, using the appropriate "action verbs," with the assumption that while some lower-order skills may be asked of students, higher-order skills are preferred (see more details in Chapter 2).

In this age of accountability, there is a great deal of focus on SLOs. In fact, on many campuses, living hidden among the bushes they share with the feral cats, are angry trolls who exist only to eviscerate instructors' stated SLOs. They sleep on uncomfortable cots, with dirty blankets, and use a thesaurus for a pillow. They play an unpleasant game, "Reword your Student Learning Objectives," abiding by obscure rules known only to them. There is no point in fighting the trolls. Make your best attempt, then reword as directed.

Course Policies. It is literally impossible to foresee all possible issues that can arise with a class (which is part of what makes teaching fun), but it is helpful to spend some time thinking about your personal policy on:

- Students arriving late to class: Do you care? Some instructors don't mind, and others go ballistic. It is helpful to structure classes so that students will be sad to miss material. Students may join synchronous virtual classes easily. This is generally less disruptive than watching students stagger over scooters and lunch boxes in an unsuccessful attempt to silently reach their physical seat. Taking roll or doing electronic surveillance at the beginning of each class session is time consuming but will encourage students' timely arrival.

- Students leaving class early: Instructors might be more worried about this issue. One instructor, while being peer evaluated, was teaching so utterly terribly, students got up in the middle of class and left in complete frustration. The poor man became so unnerved by this, he ran out of the classroom to follow his students, commanding them "Come back!!!!" They did not. Students may exit virtual classes early because technological difficulties bounced them off or because complete boredom compelled them to hit the "x"—you may never know.

- Students eating in class: Many universities have rules about food in classrooms, but these are the types of rules that are often broken, sometimes for great reasons. A small class potluck at the end of the semester can be fun. On the other hand, watching students eat during videoconferencing is significantly less festive. Instructors can request students participating via Zoom not engage in distracting activities like eating.

- Students using cellphones in class: Some instructors embrace these ubiquitous devices and require students to access information or respond to quiz questions via cellphone. Others ask all students to place their devices in a basket for safekeeping during class time. Yet others have devised creative torture procedures in the event a student's phone rings during lecture. You can be assured that students will enter the classroom with cellphones and will probably want to use them during class time. Do you care? If you do, state this in the syllabus, and indicate consequences for use.

- Students ghosting virtual classes: To re-create the unpleasant aspects of being a radio DJ, try delivering a snappy lecture to a computer screen blank except for names or still photographs, and no sound except your own voice. Instructors can ask students to show their live video faces, to ensure some degree of attention, but 100 percent compliance should not be expected.
- Students plagiarizing: It's going to happen, and lying will be involved. Electronic systems to detect plagiarism are helpful, and communicating to students ahead of time that materials will be run through a plagiarism check can reduce problems. Definitely have a policy in place regarding how plagiarism will be documented and punished, following departmental or university guidelines. Always document plagiarism so that students cannot complete their degree surfing on a wave of consecutively forgiving instructors.
- Students cheating: It's going to happen, and lying will be involved. If at all possible, construct your class so that cheating is unlikely. It's easy for students to cheat when they are packed like sardines next to fellow students taking a high-stakes multiple-choice examination. It's much harder for students to cheat when they are working on motivating, creative, self-fulfilling projects. Think through your policies on typical forms of cheating (turning in identical papers, glancing at others' exams, using unauthorized external sources of information) ahead of time, in consultation with departmental or university guidelines.
- Students being disabled: It is estimated that approximately one in five college students has some sort of disability. Colleges typically have student disability offices with many resources for students. It is a violation of federal law to deny disabled students accommodations.
- Students becoming ill: To avoid receiving lengthy emails from students describing the timing and coloring of their vomit, you might try either a "no mandatory attendance" policy or flexibility, so that students may miss a small number of classes with no penalty.

- Students' lives becoming irreparably altered: Think through how you might deal with the more common scenarios: a student is put on pregnancy bedrest, a student gives birth, a student is deployed, a student's work hours are changed, a student loses access to daycare, a student suffers a traumatic incident. Explore policies for giving a grade of "Incomplete (I)," with the clear-eyed understanding that a number of students can develop quite creative fantasies about how it would be reasonable for them to earn an I.

Course Schedule. After you have crafted the essential description of your course and created Student Learning Objectives, you can construct the course calendar. If you are teaching a synchronous class, begin by marking out each day you will meet face-to-face (either literally or virtually) with students. Note all official university holidays and breaks, along with your own scheduled work and personal absences for the term. For a course meeting more than once per week, particularly the first time you teach a course, it is most efficient to schedule topics by week rather than by day. Consider labeling Week 1 "Introduction" and Week 15 "Wrap up" (assuming a 15-week term) to build in flexibility.

The first time you teach a new class, constructing a course schedule can be quite intimidating. There is often the inclination to "schedule as you go," but this tends to be unfair to the students and more stressful, in the long run, for the instructor. Work backwards. First determine your Student Learning Objectives. Then decide how you will know students have learned those objectives. Select the number of assessments you will build into the course and place them in the course outline. Then construct topics surrounding those assessments. For example, if you decide to administer a quiz every two weeks, assign topics for the previous two weeks such that a quiz could reasonably determine students' learning of those topics. For the first time teaching a course, covering fewer rather than more topics reduces stress levels and the probability of having to madly rush through the end of the term.

Consider building into the syllabus a few entire sessions markedly different from the rest. If the course is comprised primarily of student presentations, consider adding in a few more formal lectures, a guest speaker panel, or perhaps a field trip. If the course is comprised primarily of more traditional lectures, consider adding in some relevant videos, perhaps a learning game, or other active learning activities. Variation in information delivery keeps student interest higher, and gives you small breaks in routine, to more effectively avoid instructor burnout (see more details in Chapter 5).

A few more tips for student-friendly course scheduling include the following:

- Avoid making any reading assignments due before students can be reasonably expected to acquire the textbook. It is dispiriting for students to join the first day of class, view the syllabus, and realize they are already "behind."
- Watch for breaks. Scheduling a large examination immediately before or after a break wreaks havoc with students' sometimes complicated travel plans and leaves more conscientious students obsessively studying rather than actually being able to take a break.
- Spread readings, activities, and assessments as evenly as possible across the term. Assessments are designed to give students feedback regarding their progress (see more details in Chapter 3), so earlier and more frequent assessments are more helpful. Scheduling few assessments other than a high-points paper and a final, all due at the very end of the term, gives students the opportunity to lull themselves into dangerous complacency.

Be crystal clear about dates for important assignments and examinations, including the final examination if you are holding one. Repeated and clear guidance on deadlines, including times (8 a.m.?, beginning of class?, end of class?, 5 p.m.?, midnight?) can markedly decrease hassles at the hectic end of the term.

The traditional last sentence in a syllabus course schedule is some variation of "Dates and topics are subject to minor changes, as needed." This protects you in the event you need to modify the pacing of content as you progress through the term. It is best, however, to not change important assignment dates or examination dates unless absolutely necessary.

Example shell course schedules are given in the Supplement.

How Do I Begin to Prepare My Syllabus?

In constructing a fresh syllabus, first gather as much information as possible. Will the course be offered once per week? Twice? Three times? Is a blend of in-person and online instruction allowable? Is the course designed to be a pure online experience? Collect syllabi for the same course from other instructors, both at the same campus and other campuses, if possible. Many colleges and universities have boilerplate language required in all syllabi, involving plagiarism, copyright policies, and the like. Specific departments may also have requirements, including information about Student Learning Objectives. (Warning: Do not assume any syllabi you gather are actually compliant with current department or university rules.)

Inquire about department-level and university-level requirements for courses and their syllabi each year, as decisions are made or remade frequently.

When Should I Prepare My Syllabus?

Ideally, you should begin to prepare your syllabus several months before the beginning of the term. This gives you time to gather relevant information, select the textbook and other sources or equipment your students will need, and think carefully about the experiences you want to create for your students. In real life, it is not uncommon to be notified of a course assignment with significantly less lead time. Even with a weekend's worth of notification, it behooves an instructor to begin the class with a clean and engaging syllabus. Your students need never be privy to the number of crying jags and quantity of BBQ-flavored chips required to generate said document.

How Should I Format My Syllabus?

College campuses are working to increase inclusivity at multiple levels, including modifying physical spaces, improving technological compatibility, and examining academic policies and procedures. Individual instructors are also strongly encouraged to consider inclusivity when selecting topics, assignments, and assessment methods (see more details in Chapters 2 and 3). To increase accessibility for visually impaired students who are using assistive technology to read documents, correct demarcation of document headings is essential. Best practices would have instructors be sure that all documents presented to students (slides, assignments, examinations) have correctly marked headings. But at minimum the syllabus should be accessible. Check your particular word processing program to evaluate and increase accessibility.

WHEN SHOULD I GIVE MY STUDENTS THE SYLLABUS?

Most college courses are now linked to some sort of learning management system (LMS), which is an online portal hosted by the university. Instructors use the LMS to communicate with students via announcements, to organize information via file sets, and to provide feedback on assignments and other methods of amassing points. Students use the LMS to learn about the course, view materials, submit materials, and view feedback. Popular LMS are Canvas and Blackboard. A first-time instructor, particularly a fresh adjunct, would be forgiven for trying to avoid mastery of these somewhat ponderous systems and keep communications to students as low-tech as possible. However, all instructors should work to meet the minimal standards of university-specified instruction. Students expect to gather important information from their instructor via LMS, so loading up on a venti caffeinated beverage and completing the online tutorial offered by the university is a worthy investment of time.

Ideally, the instructor would post the syllabus in the special section of the LMS designated for that before the first day of class. This allows students to take a look and become energized and ready for the first day of class (or recognize that the course content or pacing is a poor fit for their current term, and prompt them to drop the class).

For face-to-face classes, it is a good idea to bring enough paper syllabi for all students the first day, in the event that students did not think to look in the LMS beforehand. The typical face-to-face university class is packed to the rafters the first day of class, with anxious students trying to "crash" the course (e.g., get added to the roster). Bring plenty of extra syllabi, even for those who have no hope of actually being admitted to your roster, so that all students can at least feel included and part of the conversation that important first day of class.

Should I Give a Syllabus Quiz?

With increased attention given to syllabi in recent years, including a drive toward standardization of syllabi across the university and a near obsession with Student Learning Objectives, many university Centers for Teaching Excellence recommend that instructors have students complete a "syllabus quiz" very early in the term. The quiz presumably pressures students to read and memorize policies and procedures for specific courses. Students' failure to read and understand the syllabus is so common that there exist probably thousands of "Read the Syllabus" memes on the internet. A straightforward and sensible syllabus should eliminate the need for students to spend time demonstrating mastery of convoluted course procedures and allow them to proceed immediately to mastery of more universal and likely more interesting actual course content.

Revising the Syllabus

It is significantly more soothing to both instructor and student if a syllabus is constructed with enough flexibility that minor revisions in timing, content, or procedures within the term can proceed without formally revising the syllabus. Listed topics, in particular, should not be hugely generic (e.g., "inferential statistics" listed each week for 15 weeks in an Inferential Statistics course), but broader topics labels such as "Introduction," "Practical applications," "Guest speaker," and "Wrap-up" can be quite helpful and allow minor pivoting throughout the term.

Those lucky enough to teach a course more than once will benefit from thoughtfully revisiting the syllabus each term. At the point in the term when it becomes clear that too few or too many topics are listed, timing of quizzes seems awkward, additional drafts of papers are necessary, and the like, make a record of that in the syllabus to help you plan for the subsequent term. These notes help your memory, reducing the need to retroactively recall unpleasant dramas of the previous term while hurriedly creating a new syllabus for the next term.

Those lucky enough to teach a course for a multitude of years should set aside a chunk of time every several years to "pause" and reconsider the entire syllabus with fresh eyes. It is common for instructors to add a sentence or two to the syllabus every time they experience a unique incidence of cheating (e.g., "no iWatches allowed during examinations") or other disruptions (e.g., "Pretend farting noises will not be tolerated"). Beware the serial accretion of loosely related rules and commands. If, after a number of years, it appears that a half page's worth of prohibitions against student "whining" or "disrespectfulness" or the like has burgeoned upon the syllabus, it may be time for introspection as to why so many such incidents are repeatedly popping up. Said introspection should involve the content and structure of the course, not the precipitous decline of American civilization.

Brilliant Choices

Most of the details above involve *what* information needs to be included in a syllabus. Keep an eye on *how* that information is presented as well. As a point of first contact between you and the students, students will be reading carefully to get a sense not only of the class, but also of your personality. The use of warm and welcoming language in the syllabus can relax and motivate students and improve the learning environment. While remaining professional, a bit of humor (maybe a relevant little cartoon?) can be fun. Expressions of compassion (rather than "absolutely no absences will be tolerated" how about "sometimes emergencies occur, but otherwise please do your absolute best to attend every class") are welcoming. And expressions of enthusiasm (Are you excited to be teaching the class? Say so.) are helpful. Your presentations and assessments will show your own unique style and passions. Let a bit of those be revealed in the syllabus.

Ghastly Blunders

The syllabus is the point of first contact with students, and instructors would do well to not squander this important opportunity. In broad terms, a good syllabus not only details the content and procedures for a particular course but does so using language that allows instructors to begin to establish credibility, motivate students, and create an inclusive, supportive teaching atmosphere. With these goals in mind, be sure not to:

- Use grammatically incorrect language or sprinkle your document with typographical errors. (Blunder: You are demonstrating to students you are in no position to correct their papers or other written submissions.)
- Provide warning language, suggesting the majority of students will fail the class. (Blunder: You are demonstrating to students you have little faith in their ability to persevere or succeed.)
- Suggest that your particular class is more important or more difficult than the students' other courses. (Blunder: You are demonstrating to students you lack understanding of students' complete academic and home lives.)
- Indicate that any expression of student concern or dissatisfaction will be discounted and possibly punished. (Blunder: You are demonstrating that while you may wish students to learn and modify behavior based on their experiences, you are not open to doing so yourself).

Puzzlers For Your Consideration
Case Study 1: You fall hopelessly behind by the third week of the term and are thinking of changing the syllabus to cancel three of the six papers assigned.

Case Study 2: You feel sorry for students by the end of the term, and want to change the syllabus to move your final up to the last week of class, to give them more time to study for their other examinations.

Case Study 3: Week 5 of the term, you become a victim of student mutiny. In the middle of class, one of the more forthright students explains to you that you are unreasonable in your course expectations, and a number of other students nod their head in agreement.

Chapter 2

Instructor Presentation

In the context of teaching a college course, academic freedom means you can choose what to teach and how to teach, using your best professional judgment. You should be able to teach controversial topics and use unconventional teaching methods, without reprimand from administrators, as long as the topics are relevant to your course and the teaching methods are effective. You are not cleared for sipping margaritas poolside during class time, waving your hands dismissively, and shouting, "Academic freedom!" Nor does this give you permission to try a fresh approach to grading involving the dartboard at your favorite pub.

In practice, there may be less than complete latitude in terms of topics to cover in particular courses, due to accreditation constraints, mandatory comprehensive examinations, or desire for consistency across multiple sections of a course. In addition, courses with certain designations (General Education, for example) may have requirements for certain types of assignments (iterative writing assignments with a certain word limit, for example). When taking on a course new to you, it is important to inquire about any department- and university-specific regulations for topics to be covered, teaching procedures, or assessments to be assigned.

Selecting Topics

The first time teaching a course new to you, probably the most efficient way to select topics is to peruse a few current, straightforward, relevant textbooks and look for common chapter themes. Even without assigning your class a particular textbook, you can use those resource materials to identify which topics "the field" deems important. Rarely would you be obliged to cover the entire content of any textbook. Select, using your judgment, the most important topics and go from there.

Bloom's Taxonomy

Once you have made initial decisions regarding broad topics, you may begin crafting lectures, activities, and assessments for students. As you proceed, it is helpful to think about your deeper purpose for teaching each particular topic. One way to structure your thinking is to refer to Bloom's Taxonomy of cognitive skills. Educators are in agreement that there are six levels of increasing complexity, but the exact language can vary. Associated with each level are "action verbs" the trolls demand be used when writing the Student Learning Objectives found in your syllabus.

Bloom's Taxonomy

Bloom's Level	Alternate Label	Action Verb Examples
Evaluation	Creating	critique, justify, assess
Synthesis	Evaluating	design, propose, construct
Analysis	Analyzing	analyze, compare, contrast
Application	Applying	calculate, interpret, determine
Comprehension	Understanding	describe, classify, explain
Knowledge	Remembering	list, define, identify

Knowledge. At the bottom of the hierarchy, knowledge is defined as the most basic of cognitive skills. Certainly students will have to be able to remember and define certain concepts. But requiring students to simply memorize definitions, for example, does not allow them to deeply engage with material. The best college-level instruction pushes students to think more deeply and creatively about topics, increasing the probability of genuine understanding and retention. Example examination questions for each level of Bloom's taxonomy, focused on the topic of research design, are given in the table below. The example knowledge question requires students to simply memorize and report back basic differences between types of research design.

Evaluation. At the top of the hierarchy, evaluation is defined as the most complex of cognitive skills. At this level, students not only know basic concepts, they can compare and contrast them, and work with them creatively. The example evaluation question requires students to know not only basic differences between types of research design, but also the advantages and disadvantages of each. It further asks that students discern their preferences and be able to explain, using scientific terms, why they have such preferences.

Despite your charming lectures and engaging activities, a great deal of what you teach to students will be lost from their immediate memory as soon as the final examination is completed and the final paper is written. But a small set of facts may remain, and more important, procedures for relocating those facts may remain. Higher-order skills, such as analyzing, evaluating, and creating, if practiced assiduously in your class, may remain as well. Challenge yourself to consider what and how much you would like your average student to remember five or ten years from now. These moments of introspection can be a time to awaken to the profound privilege and power of teaching.

Bloom's Taxonomy Example Examination Questions

Bloom's Level	Example examination question
Evaluation	Indicate your preferred general form of research design and why this is your preference. Justify your selection using scientific reasoning.
Synthesis	Describe a true-experimental research design that would be ethical, feasible, and relevant to an understanding of the consequences of unplanned pregnancy.
Analysis	Compare and contrast the advantages and disadvantages of a nonexperimental versus true-experimental research design.
Application	Describe an example of a quasi-experimental study detailing the consequences of unplanned pregnancy.
Comprehension	Consequences of unplanned pregnancy would most likely be made clear using data from _____ studies. a) non-experimental b) quasi-experimental c) true-experimental
Knowledge	If a researcher does not manipulate the "independent variable," she would be using a _____ design. a) non-experimental b) quasi-experimental c) true-experimental

PLOT TWIST!

In the United States, March 2020 brought with it a terrible pandemic and subsequent sudden and most likely permanent shifts in public education. In the middle of the spring term, the vast majority of college instructors gathered up their teaching materials from the office and retreated to their home, abruptly modifying their teaching content and presentation modality, often within a week's time. Instructors who swore they would die on a hill before teaching online were teaching online. A new vocabulary, including terms like synchronous, asynchronous, Zoom, YouTube, and lockdown browser were acquired, along with new and colorful swear words. Today, all instructors need basic knowledge of most of these terms; at-home private cursing is completely acceptable and, in fact, expected.

In-person. In-person instruction involves a physical classroom, with student and teacher bodies breathing and talking and listening together for set periods of time throughout the week. What this will look like post-pandemic continues to be in flux for the majority of universities.

Synchronous. Synchronous instruction is virtual instruction, with the instructor and students meeting together at set times, often using Zoom or other videoconferencing software packages. Classes can proceed relatively similarly to in-person classes, with the instructor lecturing or structuring other activities, and students responding (or not) in real time. Student bodies are no longer visible. Instead, their little faces stack up on the computer screen like a strange version of the *Brady Bunch* opening credits.

Asynchronous. Asynchronous instruction is also virtual instruction. Another term for asynchronous instruction is online instruction. In this case, the instructor creates and organizes materials for the students to learn, posts it on the LMS, and students work through the material on their own time. The instructor can communicate with individual students via email, telephone, Zoom, or discussion boards, but the instructor does not interact with the entire class simultaneously.

Hybrid. Hybrid instruction involves a mix of in-person and virtual experiences for students. One variation of this is the "flipped classroom," with students attempting to master material in their own time, reading materials, watching videos, and the like, posted on the LMS, then meeting in-person with the instructor and fellow students to ask questions, do activities, or perform other tasks better suited to real-time face-to-face interaction or real-time virtual interaction.

Zoom. The videoconferencing application Zoom surged in use with the onset of the pandemic. Extended use is physically and mentally exhausting (hence the term Zoombie), but it does allow a semi-effective transformation from in-person to virtual instruction. A few tips:

- Practice Zooming with a friend before leading class. If you are teaching face-to-face, it is a good idea to scope out the physical classroom before the first day of class. Similarly, if you are teaching virtually, get to know your virtual classroom before the first day. Essential skills to master are scheduling a Zoom session, muting / unmuting the microphone, starting and stopping your video, sharing a document, recording a Zoom session, and exiting a Zoom session.

- If you are teaching face-to-face, strive to embrace your theatrical acumen. If you are teaching via Zoom, you are now a movie star! Get ready for your close-up. Invest the time to select a proper location for your computer. Find a spot that provides an interesting background (although "green screen" type backgrounds can be used) and a good angle for what, if you are normal, you will decide is your decidedly unattractive face. Consider a prop or two. Maybe you will always use the same hilarious coffee cup. Will you wear a teaching cap? To amuse my somewhat traumatized students and myself in the immediate pandemic-forced transition to Zoom, I took to teaching with my taxidermied grey fox by my side. He had different outfits for different days, including one week where he tried to pull off gangsta style. It wasn't a good look for him.

- Build in breaks, if at all possible. Face-to-face teaching involves walking to the classroom, walking back, visiting the restroom. Those moments are refreshing and energizing. If you are scheduling Zoom meetings with portions of the class during the regular 10:00–12:00 assigned time, rather than schedule a 10:00–11:00 then a 11:00–12:00 Zoom, schedule meetings 10:00–10:50, and 11:00–11:50. Using those ten minutes to do a few jumping jacks between sessions will really be helpful.

- Be crystal clear when you have exited Zoom. Novice users have a tendency to swear like sailors in relief after finishing Zoom sessions. Novice users also have a tendency to misunderstand when they have in fact actually finished the Zoom session. My dean forgave me when I let loose a few f-bombs "after" a terrible Zoom meeting, but not everyone may be so forgiving.

CRAFTING LECTURE NOTES

No matter your decisions in terms of topics to cover, depth of coverage, or modality of presentation, you generally can count on writing lecture notes to guide at least some of your presentations for your course. An important fact to remember is that these lecture notes are your private documents, so create them to maximally buttress your presentation without worrying what they might look like to others.

Lecture Notes as Script. Create your lecture notes so that they look more like a play script than an academic paper. Do not write full paragraphs of content in your lecture notes. It will be difficult to capture that level of complexity on the fly while teaching a class, and you may become tempted to read the material word-for-word to the class, which is possibly the single best way to deaden the class energy. Instead, write your notes so that they are a simple outline of material you wish to cover, with each major point supported by PowerPoint slides or other visual displays you share with the class. A few tips:

- Use larger font sizes for your lecture notes if that eases your efforts while teaching.
- If you are worried about correctly pronouncing a word, spell it out phonetically. In capital letters.
- If you have relevant hilarious jokes or relevant stories, have no shame in jotting them down. (The canned joke routine is only embarrassing if you have students in your class the second time around, and if they are back, they probably weren't paying much attention the first time around.)
- Write "stage directions" to remind yourself to speak slowly, to ask the class questions, and to breathe. Note approximate break times.

Pacing: Too Fast or Too Slow. Novice instructors typically speak at a swifter pace than they anticipate when they present to a class. It is reassuring to begin a class with a bit more material ready for roll-out than you think you will need. It is difficult and may not always be possible the first time teaching, but if you can stay about one week ahead of the class in your lecture notes and teaching support materials, you will sleep better at night.

And just as it is a great idea to always have on hand a few basic ingredients in the home pantry for an "emergency dinner," it is a great idea to always have on hand a few "emergency" classroom activities. You can break these out if you suddenly feel overanxious or befuddled, face sudden technical details, or somehow finish your material at 10:20, with a class end time of 10:50. A generic "two-minute" paper (*Describe the concept in three concise sentences*) or a quick "pair-and-share" (*Explain the concept, in your own words, to your physical neighbor/Zoom breakout room members*) plus class sharing time afterward can get you out of a bind. The trick is to act as if this activity is an experience you had planned all along, and not something you are hysterically grasping for because you forgot to take your Xanax. For credibility, you might choose to place your emergency activities at the bottom of each set of lecture notes.

Revising Lecture Notes. It is good general practice, and extremely helpful if you will be teaching a course again, to revise your lecture notes and other supporting materials as soon after class as you can manage. Did you find a typographical error in a PowerPoint slide? Correct it immediately. Did a section of lecture take much longer or shorter than you anticipated? Note that. Was a section particularly easy or particularly difficult for your students? All these nuggets are good to remember if given the opportunity to teach the course the next time around. If you wait until general prepping at the beginning of the next term, many of these more detailed memories will be gone.

SLIDES

In the majority of college classrooms across the United States, instructors spend at least part of their instructional time flashing slides (PowerPoint is a common format) upon a physical screen or sharing slides in Zoom sessions. It is also possible to record yourself narrating your slides and post the video for students to watch asynchronously. Like any other type of hard-earned writing, instructors can become attached to their slides, and want to show them for no other reason than they worked hard to create them. It's best to avoid dogged attachment and be discriminating in creating each fresh slide. A few general tips for creating compelling and effective slides (see Supplement for more examples):

- Avoid presenting entire sentences, morphing into entire paragraphs, crammed into increasingly small font sizes. Dense text encourages instructors to read from slides, word for word, which is hopelessly boring for everyone involved. If you ever hear yourself saying "I know you can't read this, but . . ." destroy the slide immediately.

- Instead, use bullet points to structure material. Consider graphical representation of some of your concepts. For ease of readability, pick the smallest acceptable font size and stick with it.

- Be pristinely consistent in your use of heading and subheadings. It can be intimidating but overall helpful to imagine you are writing a textbook. What will the "chapter headings" look like? What font size and type will you use? Keep that format for all "chapter headings." What will the major "sections" of the chapters look like? Make the font size smaller but retain the font type. The use of more than three indentations looks messy.

- Color, animation, video clips, cartoons, fades, and the rest of the bells and whistles are fun but can be distracting to focused students. Be sparing in your use of special effects, but certainly use them if they illustrate the principle at hand.

- Like the adage "Dance like no one is watching; email like it may one day be read aloud at a deposition," remember that your slides can become a permanent record of your teaching prowess. It can be a good idea to invoke another adage: "Is it true? Is it helpful? Is it kind?" Ask these questions of each and every slide you create.

- Similarly, it is absolutely critical that each and every slide be grammatically correct, (1) because you are the instructor, and (2) so that you have at least a tiny bit of street cred if you are going to turn around and critique students' writing skills. Proofread until you go blind.

- Recurring themes in slides can be helpful for student learning. Possibilities include showing a summary of learning goals as a first slide every class period, every week, or at the beginning of every new section of content. Some instructors begin each class with a relevant quote. You can ask your students on the first day of class what questions they have about the material to be covered in class, and harvest relevant questions for an introductory slide. For example, in an Introduction to Psychology class, clinical psychology content could begin with a student-generated question "Do you have to lie on a couch to get therapy?" If the course revolves around a taxonomy, cycle, or series of epochs, repeatedly presenting that generalized structure, highlighting progress as the term proceeds, can be motivating and orienting.

Student Access to Slides. If you are presenting slides synchronously, consider making them available to the students before you begin speaking. If students have access to your slides as you teach, their notetaking burden is reduced. Particularly if you are presenting complex notation, formulae, and the like, it is important for students to have correct versions, rather than have them rely on carelessly transposed mishmashed notes, taken during class.

ACTIVE LEARNING ACTIVITIES

Research indicates that students are able to maintain attention for about 20 minutes. If you think you are imagining students' eyes glazing over after a while, despite your genius slides and charming accompanying lecture, you probably are not.

Research now clearly demonstrates that the lecture-only "sage on the stage" style of teaching is less effective than the more active "guide on the side" style of teaching. For example, in a meta-analysis of 225 science, technology, engineering, and mathematics (STEM) classrooms, those in traditional lecture-only classes had lower examination scores and higher overall failure rates than those in active learning classes.[1] Particularly in this era of academic accountability and slogans about "student success," it behooves instructors to move away from pure recitation of material and toward more active learning activities, which may be employed in both the physical and the virtual classroom.

Active learning opportunities are often termed high impact practices (HIPs) because, if properly designed, they deeply engage most students, and increase their sense of mastery and belongingness in the classroom. Fortunately, many active learning activities are fun, enlightening, and frankly easier to create than pristine slides accompanied by skilled oration.

Partial-Class Period Activities. If you wish to continue traditional lecturing for portions of the class (and often this is an efficient and straightforward method of relaying information), lecture can be broken up by activities where students demonstrate their mastery (or lack of mastery) of content you have just delivered. Examples of activities you can pop into a single class session include:

- Warm-up engagement activities: Particularly for smaller classes (in-person or virtual), building opportunities for students to demonstrate creativity can simultaneously relax and energize students. Can you go through your student roster and ask each student to caption a ridiculous image? Provide a definition for a nonsense word? Can the class create a story, with each student providing a single word?
- Two-minute writing assignments: Ask students to devote a mere two minutes to reflect upon content. Example prompts are: *Define the topic at hand in your own words. What part of this topic are you still unclear about? How is the current topic related to the last topic?* Particularly for students who don't talk well on their feet but process well after introspection, this can be a helpful activity. There is no need to collect the responses, although a spot check can be reassuring. Give students the option of crafting a drawing to represent concepts, if you think that would spark creativity and engagement.
- Turn and talk: Pose a question to students and ask them to turn to a partner and discuss. This is a more personalized version of the more classic general class discussion. Particularly in large classes,

a question posed to the group as a whole may lead, in time, to a predictable set of a handful of students routinely engaging with the instructor. If all students are asked to discuss with a partner, significantly more students will participate. Pair discussions can be done in large classes, but the noise level can rise to uncomfortable levels. In smaller classes, forced conversation can loosen up quiet classes. Zoom breakout rooms allow this activity to be done virtually.

- Think-Pair-Share: Another activity for pairs, this is also helpful for those students who need to ponder before speaking. Ask students to think about a concept, turn to a partner to discuss, then ask a subset of pairs to share their responses with the entire class. Zoom allows this to occur virtually.

- Idea lineup: This is an activity best suited for a small, face-to-face class, with room for movement. Select a question that will generate a range of responses (very much disagree—very much agree; completely sure–completely unsure; enjoy greatly—despise immensely) and have students stand and arrange themselves along the continuum. "How sure are you of your career aims?" might work in some classes, for example. This activity may momentarily break up cliques of students who tend to sit together, and prompt conversations with novel classmates.

One-Class Period Activities. Example activities that may take an entire class period or a small number of class periods include:

- Jigsaw assignments: Jigsaw assignments involve assigning portions of a larger assignment to individual students, then asking them to come together as a group to complete the assignment. For example, teams may be given a set of data to analyze and tasked to create a table or figure to present by the end of the class period. In a three-student team, one student might analyze the data, a second might create a table, and a third might present to the whole class. Cooperative assignments create opportunities for students to lead and work with one another. Students fed a steady diet of only cooperative assignments can complain that they prefer getting their instruction from you, a certified expert. But introducing a small number of jigsaw assignments can be fun and can reveal students with a natural aptitude for teaching.

- Games: An increasingly popular method of preparing for an upcoming examination is to riff off the popular television show *Jeopardy!* There are a number of templates available online that allow the instructor to select categories (e.g., *Variables, Reliability, Validity*), and input questions worth differential points, along with wild cards. Smaller classes can work as teams to compete against one another for extra credit points, or some kind of physical or virtual treat.
- Field trips: The interjection of "real life" in the form of field trips, whether physical or virtual, quickly captures students' attention. An advantage of Zoom is that field trips can be imported to the screen. Could someone be persuaded to give a virtual tour of an interesting location? Could guest speakers who would never be willing to travel long distances to present to your class now be asked, instead, to sit in front of a computer for fifty minutes and share their story?

Entire Course Activities. Many instructors are constitutionally enamored of control. They may have been drawn to the teaching profession because of the pleasure they derive in thoroughly planning activities for the class, tightly controlling student outcome, all while keeping a keen eye on the clock and the calendar. The active learning activities described above remove a bit of your control. The active learning activities described below snatch away almost all of your control and place it squarely in the hands of students.

Rather than use a traditional textbook as a guide to select and order content of material to be presented, active learning courses use real-life problems as an overarching course focus. Courses structured in this manner are simultaneously markedly more engaging for student learning and markedly more difficult for instructor management. Example active learning course styles include:

- Problem-based learning (PBL): At the beginning of the term, students are presented with a real-life problem appropriate for the discipline being taught (e.g., lack of recycling bins on campus, school lunches being thrown away rather than eaten, few minority representatives on local boards of trustees).[2] Then they are asked to work in groups to explore the problem, think critically about the problem using academic concepts, then propose or even attempt to solve the problem. Such an approach very clearly answers the perennially annoying student question, perhaps not voiced but still in many heads: "Why do we have to learn this stuff?" Finding a relevant and appropriate problem for student focus generally forces instructors to become familiar with the local community, and to contact and obtain cooperation with other organizations. Teaching a problem-based learning course requires advanced teaching skills, and can be highly enjoyable, but is not recommended for novice instructors, even those very embedded in the community, because of the heightened student management skills involved. Save this for after you have a few more traditional courses under your belt.

- Course-based undergraduate research (CURE): Similar to problem-based learning, course-based undergraduate research (although graduate students can participate also) involves presenting students with a scientific problem, then asking them to explore the problem, think critically about the problem using academic concepts, and collect and analyze data to address the problem.[3] With a hard deadline of the end of term for a final report, urgent questions arise: What kind of data can be collected? Will the data be successfully collected? What will analyses reveal? Like PBL, CUREs may be best implemented once instructors have a firm grasp of students' typical interests and abilities.

Brilliant Choices

Particularly for novice instructors, a scheduled midcourse student evaluation of teaching can provide a safety valve. While in general instructors can sense mass student dissatisfaction / confusion / impending revolt, sometimes inexperienced or anxious instructors can be fooled. A formal check-in with students, approximately halfway through the course (and after students have received your feedback on some of their work), in the form of a brief anonymously completed paper or online form, can allow course-correction if matters are going south, or bolster confidence if students are generally satisfied. Administering a student evaluation form also genuinely signals to students that you care about their experiences, and welcome suggestions to improve the quality of their learning experience with you.

Ghastly Blunders

For synchronous face-to-face or virtual classes, one of the first ways you can establish your authority and provide an encouraging learning atmosphere for your students is to begin class on time. Every class period. By beginning class on time you model respect for your students (remember—they are paying money to spend time with you) and professional ethics. Similarly, end class on time. Every once in a while you might end slightly early (better to end 5 minutes early than get only 5 minutes into a new concept requiring 20 minutes of detailed description), but be careful. Students can quickly bond to earlier end times. Never ask your students to stay past the specified end time of class. Your lack of planning should not force students to be late to their next class, have to pay a parking ticket, be late to the babysitter, or in any other way suffer.

> *Puzzlers For Your Consideration*
>
> **Case Study 1:** You get halfway through a topic and it becomes abundantly clear the entire class is not sure you are even speaking in English.
>
> **Case Study 2:** You awake with a start at 3 a.m., and suddenly realize you explained a concept incorrectly last Thursday.
>
> **Case Study 3:** While Zooming a synchronous class, your dog, sitting right next to you, throws up his morning's Alpo quite dramatically, then begins to howl.

Notes

1. Freeman, S., Eddy, S. L., McDonough, M., Smith, M. K., Okoroafor, N., Jordt, H., & Wenderoth, M. P. (2014). Active learning increases student performance in science, engineering, and mathematics. *Proceedings of the National Academy of Sciences, 111(23)*, 8410-8415.

2. Wood, D. F. (2003). Problem-based learning. *British Medical Journal 326(7384)*, 328–330.

3. Dolan, E., & Weaver, G. (2021). *A guide to Course-based Undergraduate Research: Developing and implementing CUREs in the natural sciences*. Freeman.

Chapter 3

Assessment

Assessment is any procedure put in place by the instructor to evaluate student learning and achievement. Assessments can range from ungraded two-minute casual student reflections to high-stakes, three-hour, sternly proctored examinations. Much effort on the part of the instructor involves creating and responding to assessments; much effort on the part of the student involves studying for and completing assessments. The use of assessment activities that are at the same time informative and interesting benefits both instructor and students.

Why Assess?
One reason to assess students is so that you can discern their level of mastery of the course content. Students who show greater mastery earn more points and go on to earn higher final grades in the course.

But an equally important reason to assess is to provide students with feedback regarding their level of mastery of content. By definition novices, students may not be able to properly discern their level of mastery without your guidance.

Examinations

By the time students appear on a college campus, the vast majority expect examinations to be one method of assessment. Taking examinations and receiving feedback on examinations are routine and familiar procedures for most students. Examinations can take multiple forms, ranging from no-point questions asked at the beginning of every class session to low-point weekly quizzes to the epic make-or-break clock-loudly-ticking final exams. A number of choices need to be made with respect to examinations.

Example Closed-ended and Open-ended Questions

Closed-ended question examples	Open-ended question examples
A variable is a constant. a. True b. False	What is a variable?
The following are examples of variables: a. Length of fur b. Color of fur c. Thickness of fur d. All of the above	Give an example of a variable you encountered this morning.
A sample of 40 women, half of whom had children, were weighed with an accurate scale. Which of the below is a variable in this scenario? (Check all that apply.) a. Gender b. 40 c. Children d. Weight	Describe a variable you could use to measure the construct "beauty."

ASSESSMENT

Form of Questions. Examination questions may be either closed-ended or open-ended. Closed-ended questions are more difficult to write, because the possible responses along with the source question need to be crafted, but are easier to correct. A few pointers for closed-ended questions:

- The aim of an examination question is to assess students' conceptual understanding, not their ability to solve complex logic problems while under time pressure. Avoid presenting students with annoying response options such as

  a. a

  b. b

  c. c

  d. a and b

  e. a and c

  f. b and c

  g. a and b and c

- Similarly, avoid double negatives. It is impossible to not overstate this.
- Keep all possible answers approximately the same length. Students know how to game the system, and they will pick the longer, probably correct answer, if it is very obviously visually different from the other possibilities.
- A primary advantage of closed-ended questions is that they are relatively easy to grade. If you are presenting closed-ended questions on a learning management system (LMS), you will type in the questions as well as the correct and distractor answers and preselect the correct answer(s). Once students respond, the questions will be automatically graded. A faulty paper examination answer key can be privately remedied, with coffee and swearing, in your

kitchen. But a faulty answer key loaded on LMS will be irretrievably exposed once students take the examination, so careful pilot testing of any LMS examination is crucial.

Open-ended questions are generally easier to write, because students supply their own responses, but are harder to correct. In fact, a poorly worded open-ended question can leave you deeply regretful, if not hysterical, once you begin grading. A few pointers for open-ended questions:

- Be as precise as possible in asking what you want. Again, the aim is to assess students' content knowledge, not their ability to suss out your intent for a question.
- Also be detailed with respect to form. Do you have a maximum word limit? Minimum word limit? Are bullet points acceptable? Will you deduct points for spelling and grammar?
- For grading open-ended question responses, a rubric can be extremely helpful (more later). Presenting students with the rubric will guide their writing and make for a cleaner, more easily and more fairly graded final product.

For both types of questions:

- Focus very intently on Bloom's taxonomy (Chapter 2) and your Student Learning Objectives (Chapter 1). Steer clear of simple vocabulary regurgitation. What do you really want students to know? How deeply do you want them to know it? Use your most noble pedagogical intentions to guide your choice of questions.
- Aim for high "face validity" for all of your examinations. Examinations that are face valid are judged, by the naïve viewer, to properly measure the content at hand. Your choices of in-class instructional content and out-of-class assignments message to students what is important and what is not. Be sure that those concepts you have highlighted and detailed most elaborately appear on your examination most extensively. It is sneaky and small-minded to pick an

arcane detail from a text chapter you did not mention in class, just to bust students who didn't get around to reading that chapter.
- Watch your vocabulary level. Do not introduce new terms in examination questions.
- Examination questions should be as polished and pristine as your syllabus. Proofread obsessively.
- It is helpful to students if you indicate on the examination the point value for each question. This provides them with information about which questions are most important, and which to focus on if they sense they are running out of time.
- Examinations with a mix of closed-ended and open-ended questions generally provide maximum information most effectively.

Difficulty of Questions. Aim for creating questions with a mix of difficulty, but pitch the majority of questions to be truly interesting and engaging to the motivated student. Imagine the best-case scenario as you write an examination: bright students, working diligently to master the material, who want to use your examinations to show you the results of their efforts. Create examinations to please them. I knew I had succeeded with one of my examinations when I saw a student afterwards, and she told me she was so deeply satisfied she craved a post-examination cigarette.

Publisher-Provided Questions. If you are assigning a textbook, the textbook publisher may provide a test bank of possible questions for examinations, separated by chapter. Given the myriad prescriptions for good questions detailed above, it is certainly easier to use publisher-provided questions. But do pick carefully. Despite the fact that the items are generated by professionals, they may not be ideally suited for your students or your teaching style.

Number of Questions. Be very careful to not create an examination that is so lengthy or detailed or difficult that the majority of the class cannot complete it in the time allotted. This produces general outrage on the part of the students, reasonably enough, because they feel cheated of the ability to show you their level of mastery. A slightly-too-short examination is infinitely preferable to a slightly-too-long examination. If you are lucky enough to be assigned teaching assistants for your class, pilot test all your examinations with them several days before administration. You can also try taking your own examination. Brand-new instructors would be advised to ask more experienced instructors to preview their examinations.

Open-Book versus Closed-Book Examinations. Consider your choice of open-book versus closed-book examinations thoughtfully. Refer to your stated Student Learning Objectives (Chapter 1). If your goal is to train students to quickly recall information with no access to resource material, closed-book examinations are most appropriate. If your goal is to train students to process information more deeply, with access to any information they may locate, open-book examinations are a better choice. An advantage of open-book examinations is that the need to perform furtive searches for hidden cheatsheets in hats, watches, thighs, etc. is eliminated in face-to-face classes, and the need to instruct students to install modifications to their browsers is eliminated in virtual classes.

Tightly Timed versus Loosely Timed Examinations. Another choice for examinations involves time. You may choose to have a class complete an examination within a uniform time period—one hour, for example—or you may give a class a broader time frame—one week, for example. Similar to the open-book versus closed-book decision, broader time frames are ideal if your goal for students is to have them be able to produce a product or solve problems in their own time with access to support materials. Both open-book and more loosely timed examinations push instructors to create more difficult questions, at higher levels of Bloom's taxonomy.

No-Stakes versus Low-Stakes versus High-Stakes Examinations. Not all examinations need to be high-stakes closed-book grueling three-hour ordeals. Providing students with a range of examination experiences reduces pressure for everyone in the class.

- You can generate no-stakes examinations by providing students with questions, with no reward for correct answers and no punishment for incorrect answers. This type of examination gives students the opportunity to answer the questions simply to assess their own level of understanding of the material. Many instructors like to start each class session, whether physical or virtual, with a few such questions. Instructors can request that students purchase "iClickers" or the equivalent, with each student's response to questions recorded visually for the entire class to view.

- The trusty quiz is an example of a highly effective low-stakes examination. Multiple quizzes, each worth a small number of points, keep students routinely engaged with material and give frequent messages about what you deem important to understand and how well students are mastering content. Although surprise or "pop" quizzes can be employed, you may prefer to keep that aggressive, punitive side of your personality under wraps.
- Midterms and finals are examples of high-stakes examinations. If the point distribution for the course is constructed to weigh heavily on these types of examinations, failing these examinations dooms students to failing the course entirely. If it is very important that students practice successfully completing such types of examinations (perhaps they will need to take a timed credentialing examination in the future), then running students through their paces through high-stakes examinations may be a good idea.

Techniques for Reducing Cheating on Examinations. There are a number of ways to reduce (although probably never completely eliminate) cheating.

- In-class, closed-ended question examinations: Create different versions of the exam, reordering the items. In large classes, three alternative versions may be enough. Or create the impression of different versions of the exam by printing the same exam on three different colors of paper. Be sure to have students indicate somewhere on their response sheet which "version" they have been given.
- Open-ended question examinations: Ask students to connect concepts to their own individual lives. For example, rather than

prompt "What is the definition of resiliency?" you might prompt, "List three times you have exhibited resiliency in the past year."
- Virtual examinations: Much of the concern over virtual examinations is the opportunity to cheat. LMS have "lock-down" browser options that block students from surfing the web while taking an examination. But that hardly eliminates students' ability to access outside information while being tested. Open-book examinations are likely most appropriate for virtual examinations.

Reliance on Examinations. A number of instructors assess students with a midterm and final and call it a day. There are a number of drawbacks to employing such a narrow style of assessment.

- Students with high test anxiety may be unfairly assessed. College students are more anxious than ever before,[1] and there are plenty of students who have completely mastered the course content who freeze when faced with a set of questions and a ticking clock.
- Particularly if you are teaching multiple courses, your workload can become very concentrated at certain portions of the term. Grading three stacks of 100 students' short-answer responses, while you badly need to complete your Christmas shopping, is not festive.
- In addition to learning the quality of their performance on an examination, there is little opportunity to systematically gain more knowledge about each of your students. Giving students more leeway in their assessments (see below) can encourage their creativity and spark your own interests.
- Examination-only assessment does not address variability in student strengths. Some students do well with time-pressured multiple-choice examinations but write poorly. Some delight in solo class presentations but struggle with group collaborative work. Allowing students a variety of ways to demonstrate mastery is more fair to them and is more interesting for you.

Papers

A major objective of many universities is to equip students with strong writing skills. Tireless faculty in Departments of English do heavy lifting in this area, but other instructors can provide support, encouraging their students to write in their selected discipline, to use their discipline's style manual (e.g., the *APA Manual* for psychology), and to emulate professional writing. Similar to examinations, papers can take on a variety of styles; the dreaded 20-page final paper is just one variation of a theme.

Iterative Papers. If students provide drafts of a paper, receive feedback, and then work to improve their final work, this is termed an iterative paper. Particularly for such big-ticket items as final papers, requesting then providing formal assessments of drafts is an excellent idea. Required drafts are helpful in that:

- Students begin their efforts on important work earlier than they might otherwise. Due dates for drafts prompt students to work on important projects week 5 of 15, rather than week 15 of 15.
- Instructors can head off significantly wayward efforts before students have put in much time. For example, students who begin writing an independent research report with a plagiarized Wikipedia definition of "science" can be swiftly redirected.
- Peers can be employed as sources of feedback, which can be enlightening for all. Weaker students may become aware of others' strengths, perhaps leading them to join a study group. And stronger students may drop self-punishing inner dialogue, realizing the relative merit of their work compared to others in the class.
- Instructors can actually see, within the space of a term, improvement in student work, in direct response to their feedback. Instructors, in the caffeine-fueled haze of end-of-term grading, may fantasize that their carefully crafted comments on a final paper will be read with earnest and grateful hearts, and that students will learn and perform better the following term. Maybe. Or maybe they should sip their bitter espresso with the dark knowledge that the typical student will most likely never pick up or

view the final paper, or disregard the majority of comments on the paper, with the exception of the big letter at the top of page 1 or the score in the relevant column of the LMS.

- Important discussions with students about the process of creating academic work can occur. It is helpful for students to know that professionals, including instructors, also begin their important work with what is most often accurately described as "shitty first drafts."[2]

No-Stakes versus Low-Stakes versus High-Stakes Papers. Just as with examinations, papers can run the gamut from ungraded quickies to ponderously detailed 20 pagers.

- Asking students to complete a two-minute paper (Chapter 2) can focus minds and clarify thinking. You can simply look over responses but not grade them. Students who have made a steadfast commitment to never asking a question in class may feel more comfortable writing out their confusions.
- Low-stakes weekly logs, graded with a simple rubric (see below), can keep you apprised of students' progress and keep students processing their experiences. Internship / practicum / service-learning type classes are a high-impact practice because they allow students to tie academic content with real-life applications. Asking for a weekly log can prompt students to make those ties more explicit in their minds.
- High-stakes papers, like the "final term paper" many instructors assign, give students the opportunity to think more deeply about concepts and practice organizing content and writing professionally. More detailed rubrics (see below) will be helpful to both students and instructors with high-stakes papers.

Techniques for Reducing Cheating on Papers. There are a number of ways to reduce (although probably never completely eliminate) cheating on papers.

- Make use of applications such as Turnitin and SafeAssign, which are loaded on LMS. Tell students before their submissions are due that you will be using these applications, and they will know that students copying other students and students copying published work will be instantaneously identified via these computerized text databases.
- Create paper assignments that include personal reflection, fresh data collection, or some other type of effort that allows creative and unique student input.
- Similarly, develop assignments that have real-work significance and accountability. By appealing to students' prosocial inclinations, their efforts may be more sincere and rigorous and fresh.

Presentations

The majority of students dread the thought of doing a class presentation, but the majority of students can also benefit from some practice thinking and speaking on their feet. There are a number of ways you can structure presentations so that both your pains and students' pains are minimized.

Individual Presentations. Students don't necessarily need to speak for an extended period of time to get good public speaking practice. In fact, allotting a relatively brief period (5 minutes, perhaps) helps students focus on being concise. A few points:

- Short presentations lend themselves to sessions with multiple student presentations. The "we are all in this together" atmosphere soothes some nerves.
- Provide at least some kind of rubric to students before their presentation, so that they understand what they are to present. If you have a time minimum or maximum, deduct points for violating time rules.
- If you want to avoid technical troubleshooting for each nervous student, with a slightly different computer / version of Power-Point / cable / what have you, so that they can proceed with their presentation, you can consider forbidding students to present

slides and request that they simply speak to the class. If you do want students to practice creating and then presenting from slides, consider asking students for their slides ahead of time and loading them on your own computer. In face-to-face classes, students can use your computer; in virtual classes you can share their slides as host of virtual instruction.

- Just as it is highly likely you will have students who are extremely anxious when taking examinations, it is equally likely you will have students who are extremely anxious about public speaking. Be as warm and supportive and clapping as you can stomach. Direct instruction about how to manage nerves while speaking may be deeply appreciated by students. You could share some of your own techniques for reducing anxiety while speaking (see more details in Chapter 5).

- A fun variation on brief student presentations is staging interactions between yourself and each student individually, as the rest of the class watches. Could you practice a portion of a simulated job interview with each student? They could test-run their interview clothing with you, and you could put the kibosh on Shelly's excessive-cleavage interview blouse. An example enlightening activity would be for the instructor to make purposefully ignorant statements and ask students to respond in a clear and respectful manner. Ham it up a little. It's okay to play, as long as students are learning.

Group Presentations. Group presentations reduce students' pain in one way but can increase their pain in other ways. It's less frightening to share a classroom podium or Zoom screen with others. But group work involves coordination and shared effort, which may not be strong suits for all students. The smaller the group and the lower the stakes, the easier your and the students' lives will be.

- Rubrics are even more important for group presentations, because there are more opportunities for confusion. To build in accountability, allow students to grade their fellow group members for effort put into the presentation.

- Intersperse student presentations with other styles of teaching so that the course doesn't feel like one long slog similar to war: "long periods of boredom, punctuated by moments of sheer terror." See Chapter 1 Supplement for suggestions of course outlines that include student presentations.

- Consider giving students options for presentations. Yes, they could do a PowerPoint presentation to relay information. But what about allowing them to stage a skit? Paint a picture? Put on a puppet show? Create and play a video? Make a webpage? Write and perform a song? Train their dog and bring her in to show off her new skills? Could a class be enticed into performing an interpretative dance representing the Cycle of Science? Even if no one takes you up on the more far-flung ideas, just offering the suggestions will fuel creativity and interest.

RUBRICS

Responses to closed-ended examination questions are easily marked correct or incorrect, with the total number of correct responses added to create the final score. Straightforward homework assignments may be similarly graded.

But to grade responses to open-ended examination questions, along with other types of papers, you will most likely need to create a rubric. Gone are the days that an instructor reads a final term paper, makes a few scribbles along the margin, takes a thoughtful sip of coffee, a good drag from a cigarette, and writes "B+" on the top. Students expect and benefit from rubrics, because rubrics make instructors' expectations for student work explicit. Students also benefit from rubrics because they guide instructors to apply the same standards to all students, ensuring more fair assessment.

Rubrics can range from very simple to fantastically elaborate. Consider a simple rubric below.

Simple Rubric
Briefly summarize the results of the study
    0 =   Contains errors or is incomplete
    1 =   Satisfactory

Or consider a move differentiated rubic

More Differentiated Rubric
Writing clarity and coherence
    1 =   *Writing is utterly incoherent*
    2-3 =   *Writing is so poor as to have very little clarity or coherence*
    4-6 =   *Sentence structure, word choice, lack of transitions and/or sequencing of ideas make reading and understanding difficult*
    7-9 =   *Sentence structure and/or word choice sometimes interfere with clarity*
    10-11 =   *Sentences are structured and words are chosen to communicate ideas with adequate clarity*
    12 =   *Writing flows perfectly smoothly and logically*

The most detailed rubrics involve creating a matrix, with qualities to be judged listed as rows, and levels of mastery listed as columns. More detailed rubrics are more difficult to create but provide more direction and feedback to students.

ASSESSMENT

Dimension	No evidence 0	Weak 1	Fair 2	Good 3
Environmental	Lacked any mention of environmental impact	Mentioned environmental elements in discussion but did not give specific examples of how the case study considered environmental impacts	Gave one example of minimizing negative environmental impacts	Multiple examples of efforts to minimize negative impacts, such as decreased air pollution, material recycling, waste minimization, minimized energy consumption, etc.
Economic	Lacked any mention of cost, local economic benefits, etc.	Mentioned cost or economics but did not show how the case study was a sustainable example	Gave one example of how the case study met an economic sustainability goal	Discussed multiple innovations that saved taxpayer money, provided jobs, etc.
Social	Lacked any mention of social benefits	Mentioned social benefit but did not give a concrete example that pertained to the case study	Gave one example of how the project provided positive social benefits or tried to minimize negative social impacts	Gave multiple examples that community input considered, contributed in a positive way to the community, considered social equity, etc.

Consider an example of a more detailed rubric above.

Imagine the following prompt for a paper: "Discuss the environmental, economic, and social impacts illustrated in the Case Study." If you provide students with the rubric above, before they write the paper, the overall quality of papers generated is almost guaranteed to be higher. First, students would know you weren't kidding, and you wish them to address the environmental *and* the economic *and* the social impacts. Second, they would have specific guidance about how to detail each of the impacts.

For novice instructors creating brand-new assignments, it may seem overly difficult to generate a rubric before seeing students' completed work. But a rough rubric is better than no rubric. Even providing a general outline of a paper, along with maximum point values, will be very helpful to students and increase the quality of work generated.

For example, for a 100-point paper, you could create a fairly detailed rubric.

Paper Rubric

	Maximum points
Introduction	10
Arguments Pro Controversial Topic	20
Arguments Con Controversial Topic	20
Your Opinion	10
Justification of Your Opinion	30
Conclusion	10
Total	100

TIMING OF ASSESSMENTS

Students have much greater opportunity to become aware of deficits, and to work to correct deficits, with weekly homework assignments, multiple quizzes, and iterative assignments. Be very aware that this is only effective if students are actually receiving feedback from you in a timely manner on these more frequent assessments. Think seriously about grading workload, particularly if you are teaching multiple classes. Do not assign more work than you are capable of evaluating and returning promptly.

Be mindful of timing such that, if three similar papers are to be assigned, students have your feedback on the first paper before they attempt the second. It is frustrating for students to learn of your grading style and preferences late in the process of assessment. Most students work to please the instructor, so the more guidance you provide, the happier everyone will be.

Consistent feedback is the best feedback. It is difficult for students to self-correct if the first inkling they are not properly mastering information comes in week 10 of a 15-week term. Imagine the scenario of a midterm week 8 of 15, a final week 15 of 15, and a single-iteration paper also due week 15 of 15. If the instructor is a bit slow grading and returning to students their midterm results, those with poor scores will have only about five weeks to return to previous material to remaster it more effectively, while working harder to master current information, all while writing a paper.

CHEATING IN GENERAL

A motivated cheater most likely will be able to cheat around nearly every pedagogical roadblock, and it may not be worth the effort to thwart America's best future jewel thieves. But average students cheat for a number of reasons that can be addressed by good teaching practices:

- Students are desperate: Are the majority of students in the class receiving failing grades? A sense of extreme anxiety may lead to extreme measures. Providing multiple opportunities to earn points and multiple methods to earn points lessens tensions for students.
- Students feel grading is capricious: The meaning behind points earned and grades received should be well understood and accepted by students. If grading is perceived as arbitrary by students, they will be less motivated to "play by the rules."
- Students feel assignments are meaningless / busywork: The value of every assignment done both in and outside of class should be clear to all students.
- Students feel abandoned: Be explicit in your role as helpful and expert guide to student learning and relinquish the role of discerning punisher of student errors.

Brilliant Choices

If you are giving your students a traditional final examination, it can be extremely eye-opening to add just a few simple personalized open-ended questions as last questions. You can also ask these questions as a separate assignment, but tapping students' minds while taking a final, aka while semi-hysterical, keeps answers fresh. Try:

- *List four important facts you learned from this class.* Hopefully, the vast majority of students can list four facts for you, so this question is nearly guaranteed to earn them full credit. But what students list can be extremely enlightening. Do they tell you that "All statisticians are liars"? Hmm.

- *What surprised you about this class?* Once again, hopefully students can come up with something, so these are easy points. A question like this gives you insight into the expectations they brought to class, be it about you as instructor, the content, their classmates, their assignments, etc. How gratifying is it to read, over and over, that they thought they would hate this class, but liked it because the work was structured for them in a clear and consistent manner. How thoughtful one becomes, after reading, over and over again, that they thought they would like this class, but now understand that the entire field of study covered in class is not for them.

- *What is your best piece of advice for a student taking this course next term?* This is a fun question that places students in the role of peer mentor. You can ask this question to your students at the conclusion of difficult undergraduate courses and present the advice to subsequent semesters' students. To read "do not procrastinate" gives one direction for revision of future courses. To read "pay no attention to the teaching assistant" gives another.

Ghastly Blunders

Be sure to submit final course grades by the university deadline. Procedures will most likely involve electronic submission, using a system often not intuitive, so during the first several rounds of grade submission, give yourself plenty of time to pound the keyboard in frustration and cry a bit. Also allow for the completely predictable system crash during high-use periods. Students' athletic eligibility and financial aid are often tied to their grades, so it is crucial that students receive their final grades in a timely manner. Minor mistakes you make in the classroom or online will most likely go unnoticed by administrators. Missing the deadline for submission of final grades will put you on the You Are In Trouble Now list. Stay off that list.

> **Puzzlers For Your Consideration**
> **Case Study 1:** You realize with sinking dread that the 20-page paper you assigned in a fit of rigor, due Week 6, is taking much longer to grade than you expected.
>
> **Case Study 2:** You discover three identical papers written by three non-identical students.
>
> **Case Study 3:** The multiple-choice final examination you carefully crafted for your class of 50 ended up taking the students much longer than expected. Not a single student was able to complete the examination before time was up.

Notes

1. Duffy, M. E., Twenge, J. M., & Joiner, T. E. (2019). Trends in mood and anxiety symptoms and suicide-related outcomes among U.S. undergraduates, 2007–2018: Evidence from two national surveys. *Journal of Adolescent Health, 65(5),* 590–598.

2. Lamott, A. *Bird by bird: Some instructions on writing and life.* Knopf Doubleday.

CHAPTER 4

Class Management

College students are adults, and you can generally expect them to remain in their seats and not throw spit wads at one another, but some management techniques are still needed. Good class management allows students to focus more intently upon presented material and creates a positive atmosphere for both you and your students.

INSTRUCTOR APPEARANCE
Students are usually extremely interested in observing their instructors' entire appearance, from haircut down to shoe style (or down to mid-chest, if Zooming). The first day of the term, typical students will be anxiously searching for clues about the person with whom they will be spending a significant amount of time. Expect near laser examination of your entire personage.

Clothing. Instructors at most universities have fairly wide latitude with respect to what to wear when leading class; more so when Zooming. For face-to-face classes, more professional clothing on the part of the instructor can lead to more professional behavior on the part of the students. Use other instructors' appearances as a guide. Those teaching in the business school may be more likely to wear suits, while those teaching geology may be more likely to wear jeans and sneakers.

Be warned that any wardrobe malfunction will be noticed. Before every class check zippers, buttons, Velcro, etc. Many instructors keep on campus spare essential items, which might include earrings, sweaters, socks, bras, as appropriate, in the event of a wardrobe emergency.

Face. Ideally, students are intent upon absorbing the pearls of wisdom emerging from your ruby red lips. Before every class, inspect those lips and surrounds. Stray spinach in your teeth? Errant lipstick? Breakfast in your mustache? Make it a habit to spend a couple minutes in the "green room" examining appearances before going on stage.

Virtual Lighting. For face-to-face classes, lighting choices involve turning on or turning off the lights. For Zoom classes, technology provides more choices. Log into the Zoom room a few minutes before each class to check teeth / face / clothes, and signal to the cat it's almost showtime! Good lighting techniques may need to be adjusted by the time of day and weather, so learn to be flexible and responsive to ambient lighting.

Time

Whether meeting students physically or virtually (or both), the timing of activities, including begin and end times, is primarily under the control of the instructor. Careful attention to timing goes far in creating a well-managed class.

Beginning of Class. One of the first ways to establish authority and provide an encouraging and respectful learning atmosphere for students is to begin class on time. Every class period. If you find you need a little in-class settling time, showing an orientation slide or welcoming music is an option (see more tips below).

Breaks. If a class meets for more than one hour, a break is a good idea. Like children's bedtimes, it is comforting to have a fairly narrow time range for the break (for a 9:00–11:00 class, perhaps a break at 10:00), and a consistent length for the break, perhaps 10 minutes. In longer classes, some students may advocate for no break and class getting out early.

Don't fall for this. The entire class will be more dreary, and resentment will rise proportionately every minute you hold class past when students want it to be over.

Lengthy synchronous virtual classes should take breaks too. It is much easier for students to self-proclaim maverick "break time" in a virtual class. By announcing, and abiding by, virtual breaks, you can encourage more consistent attention and effort, with the promise of scheduled relief at some point.

Instructors also should take a break during the break. Instructors who stay in the physical classroom and try to rest during break will inevitably be approached by students using the time to ask individualized questions. This is nice for the students but hardly a break for the instructor. If instructors stay in the Zoom room during break, video cameras will suddenly light up and chatting will ensue. Exit the class, in whatever mode, and refresh. For virtual classes, break time is the perfect time to work on your plank position. By the end of the semester: less burnout and rock-hard abs. Win-win.

Ending of Class. Instructors will most likely be approached at the end of class by students with questions or comments they were too shy to share during class period. Plan on remaining in the classroom about five minutes after every class. This type of planning will lower your blood pressure, particularly after a hard class or an overall hard day, when you smartly finish up right on time, and you look up to see a mass of zombie students slowly approaching the lectern with the intention of eating your brains. In parallel, keep the Zoom meeting open for a few minutes after every class. Give cues for your Zoom intentions: dismiss the class and tell students that you will be staying behind for a few minutes if they have individual questions or comments.

In a face-to-face setting, students can usually suss out when one student needs to pass on confidential information to the instructor and discretely move to the back of the class. Instructors may need to take more control in a virtual setting. If one student appears to be in need of a confidential conversation, without other Zoomers listening in, suggest a one-on-one meeting with that student later in the day.

Instructor-Student Engagement

The extent and type of student engagement instructors see is likely to vary by topic, size of class, teaching format, proximity to exams, and overall class chemistry. Below are a few tips if the amount or type of student engagement seems less than ideal.

Centering a Distracted Class. The instructor provides the lead for energy in the room. Frequently, students may need to be settled before proper instruction can begin. A few suggestions for effectively calming and centering students, ideally used every class period (with the possible exception of exam days, where students may want to maximize their time completing the exam) are given below. None of these suggestions should involve extensive amounts of time and can be time-effective in the long run. A brief transition to smoothly and deliberately move from the outside world / kitchen table to classroom can prime students to listen, interact, and learn more effectively. Some of these suggestions may feel a bit far-out, and instructors should probably pick only one technique, fitting their comfort level. But the payoffs can be huge. A fully present, engaged, true community of students is more likely to be created with a deliberate pre-instruction ritual.

- Music. Particularly easily done through Zoom, a two-minute zippy song can mark the beginning of each class.
- Inspirational quotes. Can you provide students with a different inspirational quote each class session? Google is your friend. Be sure to provide quotes from a variety of voices, and not just from old dead white guys.
- Poems. Brief poems may also be appropriate. Aim for poems with nonsectarian themes of resilience or beauty or positive power.
- Noting arrival. As students settle into their seats (either in the classroom or at the kitchen table), ask them to take a moment to mindfully note their arrival to class. Instructors should do the same for themselves. Can you ponder the question: "Why am I here?"

- Meditation. English instructors have found that a brief session of meditation before writing can increase the creativity and quality of writing subsequently produced in the classroom. A welcome, a pause, and one or two minutes of silence can let distractions drop away.
- Daily dedications. Some instructors create a ritual of having students dedicate a class session to someone they admire, whether living or dead, real or fictional. Instructors can model this the first day of class, using no more than one minute to honor their selected person. This ritual works best with the number of class sessions approximately equal to the number of students, so each student can have an opportunity to share a dedication, but once only. This is a variation of "values affirmation intervention," in which students reflect upon their personal values, shown to positively impact things like grade point average.[1]
- Mixing colors. In a small face-to-face class, consider a colored pencil intervention. Each student is handed one colored pencil and draws a small circle. Each student then creates a mixed color circle, borrowing the pencil from the right-hand neighbor. Then creates a mixed color circle, borrowing the pencil from the left-hand neighbor. Briefly discuss the colors produced, sharing any emotions or thoughts they prompt.

Energizing a Lethargic Class. It is not unusual for students to sit in physical or virtual classes before instruction in utter silence. Beginning from silence, you may find yourself delivering a snappy, thought-provoking presentation, pausing, asking for class discussion, and dropping back into silence. If this happens repeatedly—awesome presentation, request for discussion, silence—here are a few things to ask yourself:

- What time is it? Early morning, post-lunch, and late-night classes often make for lethargy. You may need to get students' blood moving by literally getting their blood moving. See Chapter 2 for examples of activities that force students to get up out of their chairs. Virtual activities may not rouse students from their seats, but may otherwise be engaging and stimulating.

- Was my question clear? Sometimes students aren't answering because they do not actually understand your question. Rephrasing may be helpful. Rather than "What do you think?" you could try, "Can you give me an example of this?" "What is most confusing about this?" Or "Give a two-sentence summary of this that would be appropriate for a kindergartener."

- How are you responding to wrong answers? If you are dismissive or mocking or express even slight annoyance with wrong answers, students may become mule-like in their refusal to play the discussion game.

- How are you responding to correct answers? At the same time, if you are effusive in your praise of correct answers, once again the pressure is on, and only the most confident / obnoxious of students will play the discussion game.

- Do I know my students' names? In smaller classes, it is definitely worth the effort to learn students' names—all the students' names. If students will not volunteer to answer, call on a few by name. An understanding that the instructor knows students' names, and is not afraid to use them, perks up nearly everyone's attention and motivation level. Zoom sessions hopefully provide student names on each Brady Bunch square (although occasionally students use nicknames—it's troubling to call on JuicyBaby). Be extremely mindful of any tendency to call on only those student names that seem familiar or you find easy to pronounce. Using some sort of random number generator to call on students can keep contact scrupulously fair.

Taming an Unruly Class. Occasionally you may be faced with a room of social chatterers, who would much rather discuss the dorm drama of last night, the newest Netflix series, or essentially anything else other than the instructional matter at hand. (It's much easier for students to try to pull this off without instructor access to a mute button.) Occasionally, such classes can work mightily to let their conversations bleed into class time. A "hard start" to class time can nip this in the bud. Assigning a quiz or other assignment at the very beginning of each class will force timely silence. Or assigning a pair or group discussion at the very beginning of each class can at least turn conversation to the instructional material (maybe). If the class time runs longer than an hour, be sure to give a break, and remind students that break time is chat time.

Once in a while a dynamic may be created, such that the majority of students refuse to speak in angry reaction to the hostile takeover of one or two or three extremely talkative students. In the most toxic of situations, a single student may attempt to showboat continuously, either compulsively regurgitating content or aggressively questioning content. Novice instructors can feel obliged to be scrupulously publicly polite to the showboater, while simultaneously fantasizing private Reservoir Dogs—stabbing scenarios. It can take enormous self-control to answer what may be increasingly aggravating questions calmly, facing a sea of rolling eyes and grimaces in the backdrop. However, courtesy is due to all students in a classroom, and the less vocal students can quickly become frustrated if they believe one student is garnering proportionately more attention than others in the physical or virtual room. Given that showboating is not a particularly socially skilled behavior, subtle cues on your part may not affect noticeable change. One solution is to pull the showboater aside after class (physically or virtually), and sincerely ask for help in hearing from all the students in the class. The two of you can troubleshoot ways to share your time more evenly with all. Solutions could also involve the showboater writing down questions instead of continuously asking them in class, spending individual time with the showboater in office hours, or even developing a special hand signal you use, to indicate that the showboater should take a break from commenting for the rest of the class period.

CIVIL DISOBEDIENCE AND CIVIL OBEDIENCE
Often classes evolve to have their own moods or personaliies.

Anger. Occasionally, despite your best efforts, a single student or a small mob of students will decide that they hate you. Particularly if you teach difficult or threatening material, after a period of time students may decide their discomfort is due to you specifically, a deeply flawed and repulsive person. You might try sending some extra charm their way, or engaging in a little light cajoling, but after a certain point, the hate may simply be part of the chemistry of the class. Do a check-in with yourself to make sure the hate is not utterly justified (note: if you have an entire class of students looking at you murderously, you may be doing something wrong), but if you feel comfortable with your performance, and the hatred is isolated, accept it and move on. Teaching is an extraordinarily social act, and absorbing the energy and interest and admiration of students can be joyful. Consider the hate salt to the sweet and try to appreciate the grand diversity of students with whom you have contact.

Ghosting. Ghosting is significantly more problematic in virtual than face-to-face classes. Students can either just "forget" to attend class, or show up, turn off their video and audio, and decide it's a great time to make quesadillas. A few tips to reduce ghosting in virtual classes (which are essentially the same tips for encouraging active student engagement in general):

- Present content in a truly engaging manner. Make clear why content is genuinely interesting and why it's important to master the material (other than so that students can earn lots of points on their exams).

- Personalize contact with students. Can you randomly select a few students each session to share a picture of their favorite book / type of animal / ice cream flavor / whatever silly thing you can think of? In a smallish class, how about asking each student to pick a class session and play a favorite (nonobscene) piece of music right before class starts? Playing a brief interactive game at the beginning of each session can be entertaining as well as centering (Chapter 2).

- Do you have a mascot for your class? Pets are not allowed in face-to-face classes but may be highlighted in the virtual scene. Perhaps your Master Meowise likes to make a regular appearance when you teach. Go ahead—spend some time figuring out if he can be convinced to wear a beret. Maybe a sombrero for Taco Tuesdays?

- Give points for participation. Although less amusing than crafting cat-sized sombreros, giving points for attendance may reduce ghosting. Note that timing is important, however. It's not that difficult to show up for roll call, then silently disappear.
- Create peer accountability. Students not inclined to show up for themselves, or for the instructor, may be more motivated to show up for group members. Assigning a jigsaw type assignment (Chapter 2) may create a sense of obligation leading to less ghosting.

Kindness. One of the fabulous features of being a college instructor is that you are working with students who at least theoretically have chosen to attend your class. There are no court-mandated college classes. (There are, of course, general education courses that may feel a bit court-mandated to students more interested in focusing on a particular topic or honing a particular set of skills.) But in general it is best to assume that the vast majority of students walk into a classroom or log into a Zoom room that first day with the assumption that the instructor is competent and knowledgeable and their fellow students are trustworthy. If given the opportunity, students can show great acts of kindness to the instructor and to fellow students. Students will be more than happy to point out your technical failures ("You are still on mute") or help when you spill your coffee all over your folders. They will only laugh a little bit. Students will often gamely provide peer feedback, peer instruction, and peer support, with positive intentions. Creativity can run high. For example, when faced with a somewhat inaccurate and very anxious graduate student grader who worriedly defended his homework scorings to class while always wearing a lovely navy blue peacoat, students aggressively pushed back for half points, but also, after class, shared the idea that to boost his confidence and authority, I should purchase him a captain's hat.

Mistakes in the Classroom

Teaching is a very human process, filled with quirky connections, laughs, annoyances, and lots and lots of mistakes. Students will make mistakes. Of course! If they already knew everything, they would not be taking your class. Instructors will make mistakes. Life will be infinitely more pleasant if you enter the class with an open acknowledgment that everyone in the class, including the instructor, will be working together to learn and grow and that mistakes will be made.

Student Mistakes. Student mistakes—the number of mistakes, the types of mistakes, and students' and instructors' reaction to mistakes—are all rich with information about the teaching and learning process. Mistakes are not to be avoided. They can instead be used with great power.

If a student repeatedly transposes letters or numbers, this may indicate the presence of dyslexia or another learning disability. An instructor's identification of this issue and suggestion to visit the student disability resource center might change the entire trajectory of that student's college career. Sensitive prompting that a student visit a tutoring center, a school counselor, or a doctor, when witnessing student discomfort or misfortune, can similarly change lives.

The variety of students' reaction to their own and others' mistakes is fascinating. Reactions to a "D" on a quiz may promote apathy, anger, laughter and playful joshing, grim stone-faced resolve, blushing shame, and/or hiccupping sobs. Learning management systems now reveal students' scores electronically in the privacy of their home, rather than publicly with a shuffle of papers. But even without the shock of an upturned paper, an open discussion of how students deal with poor grades can morph into a frank focus on how to recover from mistakes. Students will most likely be very interested to hear how you deal with your own academic mistakes.

In-class student problem solving at the (physical or virtual) whiteboard can lead to the most numinous of teaching moments. Rather than interrupt to correct the moment a mistake is revealed, instructors would do well to take a chance and see if the mistaken student, or those observing, can identify the problem without your intervention. The learning process is most visible and powerful when students publicly make an error, identify the error, then correct the error on their own or with peer support. By sharing as a group the messy business of mastering material, mistakes and all, students become more clearly a community of learners.

Instructor Mistakes. Undoubtedly, you yourself will make a number of mistakes in the classroom. Prepare to deliver at least several lectures during the course of a term that make you want to slink back into the nearest cave in abject shame. Did you develop a sudden intractable stutter? Once again inadvertently interchange the words *orgasm* and *organism*? Describe a distribution as *screwed* rather than *skewed*? Invent and immediately use the word *kerfuckled*? Confuse yourself, bore yourself, or both? Embrace the failure! This is part of your personal growth as an instructor. Gently note your errors, forgive your own errors just as kindly as you forgive students their errors, and move on.

RELATIONSHIPS

Synchronous face-to-face or virtual classes are rooted in relationship. The instructor crafts relationships with students, students craft relationships with one another. There are a lot of ways things can go well. There are also a few ways things can go not well.

Student-Student Relationships. Students may enter the class pre-paired. Given the increasing diversity of college students, possibilities include parent-child pairs, siblings, roommates, romantic partners, archrivals, teammates, or some rich mixture of these pairings. If students have group work assigned, think about the advantages and disadvantages of allowing students to group themselves. Randomly assigning students to groups will most likely split preexisting relationships, to mix things up. But friends, for example, may be more motivated and driven if they can work together. When students are given the opportunity to create their own work groups, the dimensions of division can be intriguing. A linguistically diverse class, for example, may separate to each have conversations in their native language.

Do not fool yourself that the penultimate reason all students attend class is to absorb every molecule of wisdom that escapes your pores. Many students are (also) there to be surrounded by peers, make friends, or find dates for the weekend. This social element is why some students prefer face-to-face learning environments, with more opportunity to casually interact with others inside and outside the classroom. It's great to provide socialization experiences, as long as the interactions witnessed by the instructor are professional, respectful, and feel safe for all. Virtual conversations, such as discussion boards, also need to be monitored to make sure that interactions are appropriate.

Instructor-Student Relationships. With just the right mix of strong coffee, fascinating content, and vibrant students, the energy in a classroom can have a sparky sexual undertone. There is a reason naughty schoolgirl and patched-elbow professor Halloween costumes exist; the student-professor relationship has a number of connotations in American society. If you teach for more than a few years, you can expect some student crushes, with varying degrees of blatancy. Do not become overly alarmed. Do not become overly flattered. Do not encourage or act on these crushes while teaching smitten students. Because of the inherent power differential, most universities prohibit romantic connections between students and instructors while the instructor and student are sharing a class.

In addition, with the advent of high schools housed on college campuses, blended high school-college curriculum, and the vagaries of birthdates, it is not impossible that some of your students will be minors. Make it one of your professional goals to stay off the Registered Sex Offenders list.

OFFICE HOURS

Most universities have policies determining the number of office hours to be held per week. The required number may vary by the number of classes being taught, or the number of units being taught. Policies may allow a mix of face-to-face and virtual meetings. Office hours give students an opportunity to receive individualized assistance with the course material, bring up concerns regarding the course, and discuss more general issues, including academic and social opportunities on campus, career options, and the like. Despite what you think is your general genial nature, many students will be completely terrified to approach the inner sanctum of an instructor's office and speak with the Great Wizard of Oz. Most students can genuinely benefit from some one-on-one time with the instructor, so work to encourage students to visit you.

Some general suggestions to improve office hours include:

- Discuss the value of office hours in class, and explicitly encourage students to visit you. Mention that students can use the buddy-system to visit if two or more of them have similar issues to discuss.
- Actually show up for your office hours. Every week. There is little as discouraging to students who have worked up the nerve to make a visit to arrive and find your physical or Zoom door coldly shut in their face.
- Offer office hours immediately before or immediately after class times. This increases the likelihood that students will be able to fit office hours into their schedule.
- For smaller classes, convert perhaps two or three scheduled class times to appointment times. Give each student a 10- or 15-minute time slot to visit with you. A student "forced" to visit may feel less frightened than having to proactively make that decision.
- If meeting in a physical office, if you can, decorate with a few personal items. Photographs of your family, pets, and adventures will be scanned into students' suddenly perfect photographic memories and pondered during their idle hours. My "pugs not drugs" refrigerator magnet outside my office has very cheaply and effectively loosened up many an intimidated student.
- At the same time, do not decorate your office in such a manner that you can easily visualize the presence of Hugh Hefner, lounging casually in his robe. Soft indirect lighting, deep cushy chairs, lounge lizard ferns, incense, and mood music are all inappropriate.
- Unless specifically requested by a student, keep the physical door open a crack. An open door protects you, reassuring suspicious students and other faculty that you have nothing to hide. An open

door also allows waiting students to see that you are occupied but still make their presence known.

Emergencies in the Physical Classroom

While students are in your classroom, you are the figure of authority. You are at least informally responsible not only for providing opportunities for academic growth but also securing students' immediate psychological and physical safety. Prepare, before the first class meeting, for the most common of emergency scenarios. If you anticipate befuddlement in the face of stress, you could create a summary of important emergency procedures and tuck in the files you routinely bring to class.

A few tips, in the event of common issues:

- Suddenly emergent student health problems (e.g., fainting, seizures): Know how to call the campus police for assistance. Most campuses have building-specific as well as campus-wide alarms.
- Fire or other evacuations: Become familiar with procedures for evacuating both nondisabled and disabled students, particularly if you are teaching above ground-floor level.
- Ejecting students: The need to bar intruders from the classroom or eject students from the classroom can also present as emergencies. Familiarize yourself with campus policies and procedures ahead of time.
- Technology failures: Think through what you might do in the event of internet failure, power failures, or other relevant equipment failure. The solution may be to cancel class, but some thought ahead of time helps decisions made on the spur of the moment.

Brilliant Choices

A number of instructors have had success increasing out-of-class student visits simply by renaming "office hours" "drop-in hours." The relabeling makes a visit with the instructor seem less like a formal doctor's appointment and more like a casual reception. Also, making a subset of office hours virtual is helpful for students who would like to ask a brief question "in person," but wouldn't bother to take the commute and parking time for a face-to-face meeting.

Ghastly Blunders

Despite your best efforts, by the end of the term, it has become clear that only about five students in the class of forty actively participated in class discussions. They were all White male students. Next term consider the following:

- Calling all students by name, using a random number generator
- Breaking the class up into smaller groups for discussion time
- Creating some jigsaw assignments (Chapter 2) so that each student has an explicit role to perform
- Incorporating activities at the beginning of class so that students truly get to know one another at a deep level

Puzzlers For Your Consideration

Case Study 1: Immediately after class, a student approaches you and explains she needs to drop the class because her ex-boyfriend has been stalking her, and she's afraid to be at known locations at known times.

Case Study 2: You absolutely cannot master a student's name. The utterly foreign stack of sixteen syllables cannot be forced out of your mouth. Can you give the student a nickname? He's got red hair. How about "Red"?

Case Study 3: You are finishing an unwise fourth Negroni at the local speakeasy, dressed as a flapper, complete with tiara. You notice a group of your students taking in the spectacle with great interest.

Note

1. Hulleman, C. S., Kosovich, J. J., Barron, K. E., & Daniel, D. B. (2017). Making connections: Replicating and extending the utility value intervention in the classroom. *Journal of Educational Psychology, 109(3)*, 387–404.

CHAPTER 5

Tips for the Terrified or Otherwise Unwell

Teaching is by its nature a social activity, which is why it can be so richly satisfying. But it can also be deeply intimidating for the uninitiated. And even for those who step into the classroom / Zoom room calmly, everyone experiences occasional physical or emotional disruptions that make holding class difficult. Below are some tried-and-true tips for instructors feeling terrified or otherwise unwell.

ANXIETY REDUCTION
There is much that can be done before ever laying eyes on students, physically or virtually, to center and empower instructors.

Chapter 5

Before Class. Preparation is a nervous instructor's best friend, because preparation is a confidence builder.

- If teaching face-to-face, visit your assigned classroom before the first day of class. Familiarize yourself with traffic patterns, parking procedures, and campus buildings. Bring any technology that will be used for class and practice. A sure-fire way to take a hit in credibility is to have your first act as instructor involving crawling on the floor, trying to cram various cables into various holes. Inspect the windows, doors, ceiling, and chairs for potential problems, and contact the department chair if you detect flaws that will seriously impact your class.
- In parallel, if teaching virtually, practice using all relevant technology and technology options before the first day. Playing music? Sharing documents? Playing videos? Beginning class? Ending class? Practice, and practice more than once, with the understanding that, generally, nerves sharply reduce effective problem solving.

The First Day of Class. The first day of class is a high-stakes day. Initial impressions are important, and there will be quite a bit of sussing from both sides of the podium / screen. Particularly during fall term, it can also be quite exciting. There is a "back to school" energy in the air, and it is fun to capture and highlight that energy. Act excited to be the instructor! Act excited about the material! Act excited to meet the students!

- Always walk or Zoom into the first day of class with a crystal-clear, motivating, professional-looking syllabus. This document is physical proof that the class is not all about you, but is, in fact, about effectively relaying a corpus of information to the students. If it appears, from inspection of the syllabus, that the course may be rigorous, this will make the students nervous, which is excellent! Share the pain.
- A time-honored way to meet the class is to call roll. This is the first chance to get to know your students. Students might give

their name and a little known fact about themselves. Be sure to ask about preferred nicknames. Be shameless in your efforts to memorize names. If it helps to remember Mary Moth's name by imagining Mary magnificently mating a Mammoth, do so. Mary need never know.

- To reduce tension, it can help to give students the opportunity to write a little bit about themselves on a quick paper or electronic form the first day of class. An open-ended "Any other comments?" can generate student confessions about their fears of a class, their excitement about a class, confusions about a class, all of which are helpful context for a sensitive instructor.

During Class. A helpful mantra is "The best way out is through." A nicely organized class, with interesting material and engaging activities, will go a long way toward reducing anxiety for everyone in the entire room, instructor and student alike. However, it is reassuring to have a few tricks up your sleeve if, despite best efforts, you suffer a sudden florid anxiety attack while teaching.

- Novice instructors, fearful of flubbing lecture, may try to circumnavigate their worries either by attempting to memorize their lectures or by writing complete lectures in their lecture notes or on slides, then reading from these sources directly. Both memorization and rote reading will make matters worse, because the presentation is significantly less spontaneous this way and will allow the mind to disengage from content and move toward anxiety.
- Self-affirmations (written in lecture notes? On sticky-notes above the computer?) help in moments of crisis. Some possibilities: "It's not about me, it's about the material," "I am the conveyer of important information," "We are all brothers and sisters, learning together," or "The energy of the classroom lifts us all."
- For face-to-face classes, a few body hacks to consider, if experiencing a surge of anxiety, include taking a somewhat lengthy sip

of water, briefly focusing upon the computer screen, briefly gazing out the window, or briefly turning away from the class to observe the screen.

- For virtual classes, a few body hacks to consider, along with the above, include grabbing the stress ball or other quiet fiddling toy waiting for you on your workspace, or gazing at the inspiring / funny / beautiful photograph or other form of art within eyesight.
- Any active learning activity turns the spotlight from the instructor's performance to the students' performance. A well-run course should include a number of opportunities for students to actively master material while in class. But holding in place a few "emergency" active learning possibilities is a good idea. Possibilities include stopping lecture and asking students to generate a two-minute paper, or to share-and-pair, or to simply ask questions. Invoking other types of active learning activities (Chapter 2), in addition to engaging student interest and involvement, nicely work to reduce instructor performance anxiety, because you are not performing as a "sage on the stage" but rather as a "guide on the side."

Outside of the Classroom. Preparation of interesting lectures, pristine slides, engaging activities, strong assessments, and targeted student feedback all reduce anxiety. Essentially, by practicing the craft of teaching, it eventually becomes clear that you can perform the craft of teaching. Practice makes perfect, or for the new instructor: Fake it 'til you make it.

INSTRUCTOR ASSESSMENT

Evaluations tend to make all instructors somewhat uncomfortable, but novice / anxious instructors may become truly unhinged at the idea of receiving potentially negative comments regarding their teaching. Avoidance is not an option, however. Pay attention to the formal policies and procedures in place for both peer and student teaching evaluations, including the number and frequency of evaluations, form of evaluation, selection of timing of evaluation, and selection of evaluator. Within the given constraints, do your utmost to put your best face forward.

There is justifiable skepticism regarding the reliability and validity of both peer and student teaching evaluations. For example, students' ratings have been shown to be correlated with their grade expectation, and with instructors' gender, ethnicity, age, and physical attractiveness. A frequently cited study indicates that instructors who give their students chocolate before they complete the instructor evaluation form receive higher scores than those who do not resort to such a shameless stunt.[1] Despite their deficiencies, however, most universities require both peer and student teaching evaluations, particularly for new instructors.

Peer Evaluations. If you have a choice of which of several classes will be evaluated, pick the liveliest and most interesting class. If you have a choice of when peer evaluators will enter your classroom, pick a session where you love the topic and can showcase some nice lecture along with perhaps an engaging active learning activity. If you have a choice of who will enter your classroom, pick a friendly face.

Peer evaluators will look over your syllabus carefully. You may be asked to provide examples of slides, examinations, and assignments. Some universities do not require visitation to the classroom, some ask for one visit, and others ask for multiple visits. Carefully follow procedures. Although unnerving, lack of evaluations can be as problematic as negative evaluations.

Student Evaluations. If you have a choice of when to distribute student evaluations, it is best not to hand out forms immediately after the class has received punishing feedback on an exam or paper. Be sure to provide plenty of time for students to respond. Rushed students may become angry students.

Although a tricky cognitive task, try not to obsess over free-form negative comments written by single students. But go ahead and photocopy and proudly display noteworthy positive comments. Midterm student evaluations are more helpful than final student evaluations for correcting a class immediately. But final student evaluations, although occasionally painful to read and process, often have kernels of truth, and wise guidance for instructor and course improvement.

CHAPTER 5

TEACHING WHILE PHYSICALLY OR EMOTIONALLY UNWELL
Not every single time you enter a physical or virtual class will you feel sparkly, motivated, and bursting with energy. Occasionally you may have to teach while feeling vaguely ill, bone-tired, or distracted by some other element of your personal life. It's comforting to have some tricks in place, in the event you suspect your performance may be less than stellar.

Physically Unwell. If you feel under the weather, consider the following tips:

- If you suspect a greater than 50 percent probability of throwing up / passing out / assuming a fetal position below the lectern, go ahead and cancel class. Check with your department ahead of time so that you know the proper procedures for notifying students and reporting sick-leave.

- If you judge your probability to be less than 50 percent, you might go ahead and give it a go. Lecturing, for most people, takes more energy than other activities, so now is the time to bust out the "alternative activities" you have ideally developed at the very beginning of the term. There is no need to explain to the class the exact reason you are tragically hung-over. Instead, you might announce that the class period will be devoted to deeper examination of a recently presented, fairly difficult concept. In smaller classes, try an impromptu jigsaw activity. For example, in a class of twenty, divide the class into four groups of five; have one group create five new slides describing the concept, one group write a concise one-paragraph description, one group create a graphical representation, and one group write five multiple-choice exam questions. Give time for each group to develop their product, then have them present their results to the class as a whole.

- See Chapter 3 for other possibilities of quick active learning activities. For classes of any size or format, be sure any alternative activities you select will be actually helpful to students and not be perceived as "busywork." If you haven't developed your alternative activities in advance, and your impairment prevents you from coming up with something clever, go ahead and cancel class.

Emotionally Unwell. It can certainly happen that you have to walk into a classroom immediately after dropping your child off at kindergarten (painful) or college (worse), while dealing with a personal or community tragedy, or awaiting a frightening medical diagnosis. The list goes on and on. A few tips:

- Similar to the general principles for physical illness, if you suspect a greater than 50 percent probability of completely losing your "composure" / blurting out your problems and begging for mercy / crying snottily and lengthily, go ahead and cancel class. Check with your department ahead of time so that you know proper procedures for notifying students and reporting sick-leave.
- If you judge your probability to be less than 50 percent, you might go ahead and give it a go. Now is the time to deeply focus on the material at hand. Make a commitment to return to worrying or crying or raging as soon after class as feasible and treat the classroom as a sanctuary. Leave your issues behind you, welcome your students as fellow humans also struggling in this world, and make special efforts to glory in the interesting concepts at hand, and the magic of communal learning. Gently note intrusive thoughts and return to teaching material with dedicated mindfulness.
- Do you share your troubles with the class? Maybe. Your decision should incorporate the nature of the problem, your ability to discuss the problem without alarming the class, and your own and the class's personality. A quick mention that you have just dropped off your child to the first day of kindergarten and you are feeling shaky may be quirkily humanizing. Details of your recent biopsy and the statistical likelihood that you have cancer may be too much.

Preventing Burnout

A not-uncommon career trajectory for an instructor is to experience a number of years teaching with hesitant, shaking knees, followed by joyful, sturdy knees, followed by cranky, creaky knees. Teaching is hard work, and even the best of instructors (perhaps particularly the best) can find themselves a bit tired, a bit cynical, a bit resigned after a number of years slogging through lectures and papers and excuses for poor performance. There are multiple techniques for slowing the progression of burnout.

Managing Timing of Classes. Be as selective as possible in your choice of timing of classes. While many instructors have little choice in the matter, if flexibility exists, notice and request the type of teaching schedule that best fits your energy pattern across the week. Some instructors perform best with a daily teaching schedule. Others find one or two very long teaching days, with rest in between, is a better fit. Others enjoy intensive weekend teaching marathons.

Reassessing Course Material. Reassess a portion of each course you routinely teach every semester. It would be inefficient to completely revamp a course you have developed (unless it was a complete failure), but it is refreshing to polish a different section, or try a new activity, or introduce a new textbook, or revamp an assignment rubric, each term.

Broadening Your Teaching Portfolio. If you have the opportunity, experiment with teaching the same material at different levels of sophistication. Consider converting your course to be a very introductory course for incoming freshmen, or an honors course, or a general education course, or a graduate-level course. Different types of students' reactions to material can freshen and sharpen your teaching skills. Also, if you have the opportunity, create a portfolio of different types of courses to offer. Teaching a mix of popular and practical 1-unit courses, meat-and-potatoes 3-unit courses, and high-stakes 5-unit courses can be energizing. Variety is refreshing.

Taking a Class Yourself. A fine way to reconnect with your empathy for students, by remembering what it is like to be faced with foreign content, is to plunge into a course yourself. For maximum benefit, try for a class completely out of your range of experience: scuba diving? photography? pelding? belly dancing? Spanish? weight lifting? Gently

Chapter 6

The Syllabus Supplement

Puzzlers For Your Consideration
Case Study 1: You fall hopelessly behind by the third week of the term and are thinking of changing the syllabus to cancel three of the six papers assigned.

It is reasonable to think that reducing student workload would be popular. But by removing half of the paper assignments, you are cheating the students of the opportunity to earn points and demonstrate mastery of content. It is not unusual to quite shockingly and swiftly fall behind in content delivery, particularly for novice and ambitious instructors teaching a course for the first time. A more palatable pivot would be to change assignments to be more easily accomplished, but to keep point values. For example, rather than assign one paper for each of six topics, you might assign two papers for each of three topics. The first paper could be a more classic "compare and contrast" assignment, and the second could be a "apply this concept to your life" or "find an example of this concept in the popular press" assignment.

Case Study 2: You feel sorry for students by the end of the term and want to change the syllabus to move your final up to the last week of class, to give them more time to study for their other examinations.

Again, it is reasonable to think this might be popular with students. But for many universities, administering the final outside the formal final period is a policy violation. Instructors are not required to administer finals, but if they are doing so, students generally expect to be allotted the standardized time period (often two or three hours), not the shortened time period of usual class time (often one hour). Moving up final administration also reduces time for students to study intensively, without the distraction of ongoing classes.

> **Case Study 3:** Week 5 of the term, you become a victim of student mutiny. In the middle of class, one of the more forthright students explains to you that you are unreasonable in your course expectations, and a number of other students nod their head in agreement.

Congratulations! You can now check off the Teaching Adventures Bingo Sheet square "Student mutiny"! This is bound to happen at some point in any but the very briefest of teaching careers. There are very right and very wrong ways to handle a student mutiny. If the mutiny appears widespread, it is best to stop content delivery on the spot. Listen more deeply to student concerns. Try to get feedback from as many students in the room (literal or virtual) as possible, particularly those who are initially silent. Garner suggestions for revisions to course procedures and assignments. Commit to nothing. Game face is essential here. Remain in full control of the class, while channeling your most alert, empathic self. Listen deeply and ponder after class has ended. If you have, in fact, misjudged the typical student's expectations / abilities (perhaps you are using a syllabus that worked perfectly well at Stanford but is not working as smoothly at the local community college), make minor modifications without completely upending the syllabus. Could you add the opportunity to submit drafts of papers? Allow multiple attempts at examinations? Axe presentation of the last optional topic, to move more slowly through content? Wrong choices for reaction to mutiny include the following: becoming irritated or angry (suggesting you are not open to students' experience and opinions), becoming defensive (suggesting you are not as experienced an instructor as you pretend), or becoming weepy (suggesting you are hanging on to self-control by your fingernails, or perhaps a tiny bit losing it). All these reactions are completely appropriate once class is over and you have had a generous second glass of wine. But while in class, facing your students, retain and embrace your role as calm and steady leader.

EXAMPLE SHELL COURSE SCHEDULES

Experiential-centered Small Courses. If you are teaching a small class (perhaps 10–25) designed to embed students "in the field" for experiential learning (e.g., internship-type classes), see an example shell course schedule below.

Experiential-centered Shell Course Schedule Example

Week	Class topics	Assignment due
1	Introduction	
2	Class logistics	
3	Formal lecture	
4	Formal lecture	
5	Guest speakers	Log 1
6	Student presentations	Log 2
7	Check in	Log 3
8	Student presentations	Log 4
9	Field trip	Log 5
10	Check in	Log 6
11	Guest speakers	Log 7
12	Check in	Log 8
13	Student presentations	Log 9
14	Student presentations	Log 10
15	Wrap up	Reflection of all logs
Final	-None-	

Chapter 6

Sequential Topics Courses. Many courses are constructed to allow presentation of a series of interlocking concepts. If instructors are using a traditional textbook as a guide, they might lecture about topics in Chapter 1, then Chapter 2, etc. Consider the shell course schedule for this type of course below.

Sequential Shell Course Schedule Example

Week	Class topics	Assignment due
1	Introduction	
2	Introduction—Theme A	
3	Formal lecture	
4	Formal lecture	Homework 1
5	Active learning	Homework 2
6	Quiz 1	
7	Introduction—Theme B	
8	Formal lecture	
9	Formal lecture	Homework 3
10	Active learning	Homework 4
11	Quiz 2	
12	Introduction—Theme C	
13	Formal lecture	Homework 5
14	Formal lecture	Homework 6
15	Wrap-up	Homework 7
Final	Final	

Cumulative Topics Courses. Other courses are constructed to allow presentation of a series of concepts of increasing complexity, with mastery of earlier simpler topics required before moving to subsequent more sophisticated topics. "Capstone" type courses may even require students to remember and remaster content learned in earlier terms' coursework. Consider the shell course schedule for this type of course below.

Cumulative Shell Course Schedule Example

Week	Class topics	Assignment due
1	Introduction	
2	Introduction—Theme A	Mini-paper
3	Formal lecture	
4	Active learning	Draft 1 of final paper
5	Introduction—Themes A & B	
6	Formal lecture	Mini-paper
7	Active learning	Draft 2 of final paper
8	Mid-term	
9	Introduction—Themes A, B, & C	
10	Formal lecture	Mini-paper
11	Formal lecture	
12	Active learning	
13	Formal lecture	Mini-paper
14	Formal lecture	
15	Wrap-up	Final paper
Final	Final	

COMPARE AND CONTRAST

- Logs. It is common, in experiential courses, to ask students to briefly reflect upon their experiences in the form of logs, often submitted weekly (see more details in Chapter 3). Logs provide a running track of students' accomplished goals, along with hours accumulated, and give instructors insights into challenges and successes students are experiencing. Logs allow students to note their confusions, challenges, moments of pride. The opportunity for students to reread their logs and view progress throughout the term can be motivating and eye-opening for students. A "Reflection of all logs" can be a helpful cumulative experience for students and provide edifying moments for instructors.

- Distribution of points. In sequential courses, it is tempting to rely upon large examinations only for assessment. It is more interesting and equitable to distribute points across a wider variety of opportunities. The example sequential shell has one "high-stakes" assessment, the Final, but the remaining assessments are more varied and therefore possibly more interesting and engaging, and likely more valid assessments of students' achievement.
- Speed of delivery. All instructors face the conundrum of breadth versus depth when considering the pacing of delivered material. With a cumulative course, one possibility is to front load major topics, and use the rest of the term for "practice." A more conservative approach would be to move more slowly through the cumulative topics, and ensure, via minipapers and/or active learning activities, that students are on board the train before taking off to the next station.
- Drafts. By requiring students to submit two drafts of the final paper, more explicit guidance regarding the final paper can be provided. Asking students to submit drafts forces them to begin work on a high-stakes paper earlier in the semester, and models the iterative nature of academic writing. Students headed in significantly wrong substantive directions, as well as students who need more intensive help with writing, are both aided by identifying these issues earlier in the term.

Chapter 7

Instructor Presentation Supplement

> *Puzzlers For Your Consideration*
> **Case Study 1:** You get halfway through a topic, and it becomes abundantly clear the entire class is not sure you are even speaking in English.

Even without speaking, students can communicate if they are not following your lecture. Scan whole bodies (face-to-face) or just faces (virtual) for the tell-tale "deer in the headlights" look. Often instructors present complex material that will involve additional time on the part of the student to completely master, so looks of complete comprehension are not mandatory while you speak. But if it appears you are suddenly speaking gibberish to them, you may not be providing appropriate scaffolding for their later efforts. When faced with an entire class of startled deer, it can be tempting to grit your teeth and power through the rest of the period. But it is better for you and for your students if you simply stop. Finish your sentence and stop. Take a breath. In such an alarming scenario, it is human nature to quickly cast about to find someone to blame. Your students are stupid. You are a terrible teacher. Ideas like those provide only temporary relief and are likely untrue. Gather information from your students about what, exactly, is confusing. Assign a quick "two-minute" paper with the prompt "List three things you really understand about this concept. List three questions you have about this concept" or similar and study their answers. The next meeting with class, you might try a brief recap of material, an explanation of why certain concepts are important to master, or an active learning exercise to pinpoint specific areas of student confusion.

> **Case Study 2:** You awake with a start at 3 a.m., and suddenly realize you explained a concept incorrectly last Thursday.

It happens. While striving for 100 percent accuracy and 100 percent charm, human instructors occasionally fall short of this target. If your inaccuracy was extremely minor and isolated from other concepts presented in the course, you can probably just let it go. But if your inaccuracy was important (your gut will let you know: for example, the 3 a.m. wake-up) you are going to have to face the music. No need to drop to your knees, clutch your hair in hysteria, and beg for forgiveness the next class period. Simply calmly mention it occurred to you that you may not have been crystal-clear about a certain topic, and teach it again, this time correctly.

> **Case Study 3:** While Zooming a synchronous class, your dog, sitting right next to you, throws up his morning's Alpo quite dramatically, then begins to howl.

Congratulations! You can now check off the Teaching Adventures Bingo Sheet square "Dog throws up in class!!" Misadventures can occur in the physical classroom. But teaching synchronously virtually from home introduces additional challenges. The doorbell can ring. A child may request assistance. A husband may walk by in his underpants. And pets always enjoy a crowd in the event of bodily malfunction. Embrace these moments as part of the deeply human, deeply idiosyncratic nature of teaching. Introduce your class to your dog, spend a moment feeling sorry for him, maybe throw a towel over his transgression, and proceed.

INSTRUCTOR PRESENTATION SUPPLEMENT

You and Rufus have just provided your students with an entertaining story for the day.

EXAMPLE SLIDES
Below are samples of slides. Inspect them, then compare and contrast.

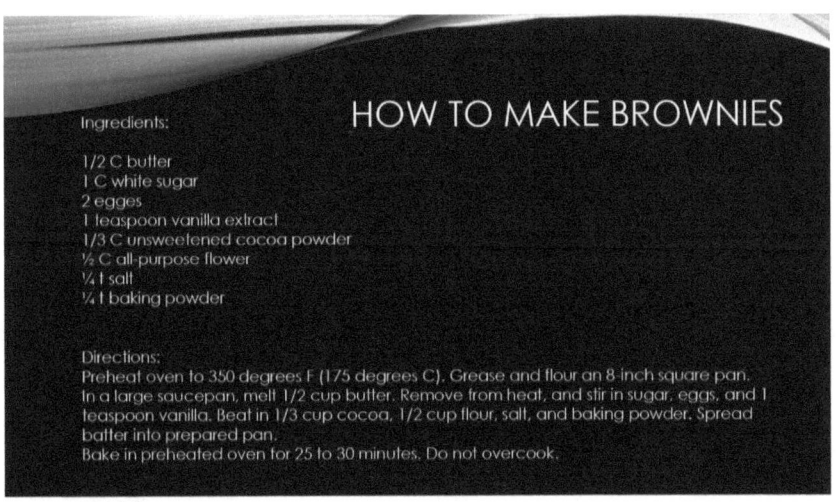

CHAPTER 7

Recipe 5: Brownies

Ingredients

1/2 C butter
1 C   white sugar
2   eggs
1 t   vanilla extract
1/3 C unsweetened cocoa powder
1/2 C all-purpose flour
1/4 t salt
1/4 t baking power

Recipe 5: Brownies

Directions

- Preheat   oven 350° F
- Grease & flour 8-in square pan
- Melt   butter
- Remove   from heat
- Stir in   sugar, eggs, vanilla
- Beat in   cocoa, flour, salt, baking powder
- Spread   batter into prepared pan
- Bake   preheated oven 25-30 min

Do not overcook!

COMPARE AND CONTRAST
- Typographical errors. The first slide "How to make brownies" has a number of typographical and stylistic errors. Note the incorrect

spelling of flour and eggs, and the inconsistent presentation of measurements (1/2 some places, ½ other places).

- Amount of verbiage. The first and second slides read like text, which makes for laborious reading and notetaking. If you want to make a complete recipe for brownies available to students, a pdf would be more appropriate than a slide.
- Style conventions. Most recipes are presented in a similar format, with ingredients listed in a column, then directions presented as text. The second slide violates typical style conventions by listing ingredients as text, which may be confusing to some.
- Slide format. The very dark formatting of the first slide is somewhat forbidding and will waste ink if students decide to print their slides. The second slide's colorful format is less intimidating but odd. The third slide is more neutral, and therefore less distracting.
- Precision. By breaking content into two slides, the "Recipe 5: Brownies" set cleanly first presents the ingredients, with aligned columns and matching measurement units. The second slide uses precise action verbs (reheat, grease & flour) in the first column, and the appropriate nouns in the second column. Note how the important admonition not to overbake the brownies pops when those words are separated from the rest of the text and italicized.

CHAPTER 8

Assessment Supplement

Puzzlers For Your Consideration
Case Study 1: You realize with sinking dread that the 20-page paper you assigned in a fit of rigor, due Week 6, is taking much longer to grade than you expected.

Perhaps you haven't even started grading yet, because the physical or electronic pile is so intimidating or because you are so busy frantically churning out lecture content to have something to say to the class three times per week. Particularly if you are asking students to write another paper this term, or if the paper is a big-ticket item (and it should be, if it is 20 pages long), timely feedback is important. If you gave students a rubric, use it to structure your feedback. There is no need to act as copy editor. If you did not give students a rubric, create a simple one, and again, give feedback just on elements of the rubric. Can you look ahead, and introduce a class session or two that does not involve heavy preparation on your part? Ease up on lecture preparation and use the time to grade the papers. Power through and make a note to not create such drudgery for yourself next time around.

Case Study 2: You discover three identical papers written by three nonidentical students.

Chapter 8

Cheating and plagiarism on papers are quickly caught with systems such as Turnitin and SafeAssign found in learning management programs (LMPs). When students submit their papers via a LMP, be sure to announce that all papers will be run through an electronic check. The three identical papers will be instantly snagged. Because you, of course, indicated consequences of cheating and plagiarism on your syllabus, bypass the sanctimonious outrage, and simply follow procedures in your syllabus. The university will provide guidelines, but also instructor latitude, for punishing those who have cheated. A typical penalty might be "0" on the assignment, with "F" in the class if any subsequent events occur. Check with the department chair to make sure you are aware of any unwritten university conventions. It is important to report all incidents of cheating to the university.

> **Case Study 3:** The multiple-choice final examination you carefully crafted for your class of 50 ended up taking the students much longer than expected. Not a single student was able to complete the examination before time was up.

Congratulations! You can now check off the Teaching Adventures Bingo Sheet square "No one finishes the exam!" If literally no one was able to complete the examination, evidence suggests you underestimated the difficulty of the examination or the mastery level of your students. It happens. Examine students' results very carefully. Were they proceeding well but ran out of time? Did they seem to get stuck on one problem and used all their time trying to solve it? Did they misread instructions, and believe they needed to write full sentences rather than use bullet points? Identify their mistakes and correct the examination as appropriate for next time. A common method of allotting points in this circumstance is to "grade on a curve." Rather than simply creating a percentage of points earned to total possible points and giving "A"s to those with 90 percent points earned or higher, etc., find the student(s) with the highest number of points earned, and make this the modified "total possible points." Calculate the percentage of points earned based on this modified number and proceed to grade as usual. For example, if the highest score on a 100-point assignment is 60 (suggesting some sort of misalignment between instructor, assignment, and students), you can set 60 as the new top score. A student with a score of 50 now earns 50/60 or 83 percent (B), rather than 50/100 or 50 percent (F). Communicate to students your modified grading procedures, but don't belabor the point. Smile and move on.

Example Rubrics

Problematic Paper Rubric: Rubric 1
Introduction
    Literature Review
    Methods
    Results
    Discussion

Improved Paper Rubric: Rubric 2

	Maximum points
Introduction	10
Literature Review	10
Methods	10
Results	10
Discussion	10
Format	50

Even More Improved Paper Rubric: Rubric 3

	Maximum points
Introduction	10
Literature Review	
Statement of problem	5
Review of previous work	15
Methods	
Participants	5
Measures	10
Procedures	5
Results	
Descriptive results	5
Inferential results	5
Discussion	
Restatement of problem	5
Summary of results	5
Connection to previous work	10
Strengths and limitations of work	5

COMPARE AND CONTRAST

- Indication of points. The most problematic rubric, Rubric 1, gives an idea of structure for the paper, but does not indicate the relative importance of each section. The overall point value for the paper is not made explicit. Rubrics 2 and 3 give points, and Rubric 3 is very clear about the total number of points that may be earned.
- Weighting of points. Both the absolute and relative number of maximum points earned are valuable pieces of information to the discerning student. Savvy students will work more intently on higher-point sections. The weighting of points is where the instructor explicitly indicates the importance of each element. Rubric 2, for example, gives the message that format is more important than substance. Unless you are teaching proofreading

and transcription skills, a redistribution of points would be more appropriate.

- Level of detail. Rubric 3 provides greater detail regarding not only the desired segments of the paper, but order and form of subsections within segments as well. More detailed rubrics allow students to focus less on how to format the paper and focus more on content of the paper. If you really have a format in mind, being explicit about that format will make everyone happier. "Ask, and ye shall receive." Or at least, "Ask, and ye shall be more likely to receive."

CHAPTER 9

Class Management Supplement

Puzzlers For Your Consideration
Case Study 1: Immediately after class, a student approaches you and explains she needs to drop the class because her ex-boyfriend has been stalking her, and she's afraid to be at known locations at known times.

Sadly, this is not an unusual situation. Fortunately, any university that receives federal funds (including both public and private universities) has a set of policies and procedures in place to address sex-based discrimination, with stalking falling under this heading. To not be caught unaware, familiarize yourself with "Title IX" policies before teaching, or at least get a basic primer from the chair of the department. If the student feels she is in immediate danger, call the police and stay with her until the police arrive. If the student does not feel she is in immediate danger, at minimum, refer her to the Title IX office on campus. Or better, connect her with that office by telephoning or Zooming or physically visiting along with her to ensure that contact is made. Thanks to offices like Title IX, you are not put in a position of determining the veracity of her claims, the level of danger involved, or how to stop the stalking. Your role is to connect students to the appropriate professionals on campus.

> **Case Study 2:** You absolutely cannot master a student's name. The utterly foreign stack of sixteen syllables cannot be forced out of your mouth. Can you give the student a nickname? He's got red hair. How about "Red"?

Or how about making a silent commitment to never call on that student for the entire term? Neither silence nor nickname is an appropriate choice. Here is a situation where you have the opportunity to publicly model for students your personal process for mastering difficult material. How does this process best work for you? Should you write out the name phonetically? Can you draw a picture? Somehow fit in some analogies? Are you just going to have to practice a lot? Have other students in the class mastered speaking this name? Ask about their process. Yes, this takes more time than using a nickname, but proper names are an important part of identity. The fact that you cannot pronounce a name may indicate that the student has a different ethnic or religious background than yours. Do not try to erase diversity for your personal convenience.

> **Case Study 3:** You are finishing an unwise fourth Negroni at the local speakeasy, dressed as a flapper, complete with tiara. You notice a group of your students taking in the spectacle with great interest.

Even in relatively large towns, off-hours contact between instructors and students will likely occur. Students work at the local drugstore where you buy your condoms. They work at the grocery stores where they carefully inspect the type of panty liner you prefer. They work at the daycare, judging your younger child's inability to be fully potty-trained. On the upside, though, it can be enlightening for students to see and understand that instructors are people too, and they live and participate in the community. This point will be driven home when they see that Professor Elmsworth enjoys wearing tiaras and a flapper dress on his off hours. Wave hello when seen and carry on.

Example Response 1
(Immediately delete the email and head for a bourbon.)
Consider the example student email below.

> **Student Email**
> Subject: Psych 100 grade
> To: Constance
> Cc: Chair, Dean, President
>
> Hey Mrs. Jones –
> I can't believe you gave me a 36 Out of 100 on Quiz 6. I studied for literally hours and those questions were crap. You clearly don't know how to teach and I don't deserve to pay money to not pass this class. The entire class should be able to take all the Quizzes over again. I have also emailed your Chair, your Dean, and the President of the University, because they should know what a terrible job you are doing and how students are having their money wasted. – Janet Smith

Example Response 2
Subject: Psych 100 grade
  To: Janet
Thank you so much for your nuanced analysis of my pedagogical skills! And how thoughtful of you to share your perspectives with my chair, the dean, and the president of the University! Were it within my purview to return your tuition fees, I would most certainly do so. I would also remove you from my "Psch 100" to save us both misery. You may not take Quiz 6, or any of the other Quizzes, again. Do not email me again or I will report you to the Dean of Student Services for harassment. Sincerely, "Mrs. Jones"

Example Response 3
Subject: Psych 100 grade
    To Janet

Thank you for your email. I notice you consistently get Ds or Fs on the quizzes, so your score on Quiz 6 should not be a surprise to you. You seem to be having a hard time mastering the material in Psych 100. Maybe Psychology is not the right major for you. I do not allow students to retake quizzes, because I find that students rarely improve their scores and it delays studying time. Also, it is not fair to the strong students who study, and study correctly, the first time around. Sincerely, Constance Jones

Example Response 4
Subject: Psych 100 grade
    To: Janet

Thank you for your email. I know how disappointing it is to study hard for a quiz and still not get a great score. Frustrating! I notice you earned similar low scores on quizzes 1 through 5. Let's sit together and talk about the class in general, and how you have been studying for it. My office hours this semester are Mondays 1–3 (in Science Building Room 301) and Tuesdays 2–4 (Zoom link here). Do any of those time slots work for you? There are still plenty of quizzes, plus the final, plus the paper, for you to pull up your grade. I hope to connect with you soon. Sincerely, Dr. Jones

COMPARE AND CONTRAST

- Avoidance. The temptation can be quite strong to simply delete offensive and abusive student emails. But particularly given that the email in question involves the deeply unfortunate cc'ing of the chair, dean, and president, your response, including timeliness and tone, is now of elevated interest to many. The more offensive the email, the more a timely and professional response will be admired. Play ball!

- Sarcasm. The majority of student emails are generally fairly civil and reasonable. This makes the occasional genuinely rude email particularly shocking. Instructors' first reaction to offensive emails often involves raised eyebrows and the squeaky haughty voicing of a few choice swear words. Fair enough. Do not commit the error of setting this down in writing. Or do so, but be very careful to not actually send the email. Sending that type of email feels deeply satisfying for only about 15 minutes, and then regret will kick in.

- Excessive justification. If a student is complaining about specific class procedures (e.g., not being able to retake quizzes), a brief reiteration of the justification of your choice is reasonable, but there is no need to go into excessive detail. Giving an exhaustive list of your teaching qualifications, reasons for your class policies and procedures, selection of quiz questions, etc., can come across as defensive and can heighten rather than dampen student outrage.

- Reflection. Rather than getting caught up in the horrific grammar / entitlement / deep confusion of a rude student email (or, after you have processed those initial reactions), take a moment to consider how the student is feeling. Angry? Frustrated? Depressed? Scared? In the example email, the student appears to be frustrated that she studied for a certain period of time, but did not see her efforts reflected in strong quiz grades. Can you reflect that emotion back to her in an email?

- Personalized messaging. It can be helpful to personalize a response email by first doing some investigative work. How is the student scoring on assessments in general? Is she doing well on certain types of assignments (e.g., group activities), but poorly on others (e.g., high stakes examinations)? What does attendance look like? At this point, is there any hope of passing the class, given the number of points yet to be earned? Personalized comments help students feel understood and can diffuse hostility quickly.

- Professionalism. It can be extremely tempting to respond to rude student emails quickly, sarcastically, and punishingly, particularly if one is feeling hilariously creative, as fueled by a few cocktails. If instructors are able to resist the urge to purge but truly cannot navigate their way to a professional response, this would be a time to visit the chair. Instructors might even show a draft of a response to the chair or colleague before exposing content to the open airwaves. No matter how boring / infuriating / confused the email, aim to respond within 48 hours, during regular working hours.

Chapter 10

Teaching for the Terrified Supplement

> *Puzzlers For Your Consideration*
> **Case Study 1:** A deeply beloved member of your family shockingly and unexpectedly passes away one week before the end of the term. You are simply in no condition to be seen in physical or virtual public, much less be expected to speak.

If you are in a sufficiently capable state of mind, check your contract for bereavement leave. If that is beyond you, simply contact the chair of the department and pass on subsequent decision making to that person. You most likely will not be ordered back into the classroom (particularly one week before the end of the term), but your students will still need their final assessments, if scheduled, and material graded, if that work remains to be done. Gently check in with yourself, and if you determine you simply will not be able to complete the term, communicate that with the chair, who can make arrangements for substitute graders, etc. It may be tempting, particularly in an altered state of mind, to cut the class short and cancel all subsequent work, or give everyone an "A," or just walk away. These types of situations are why chairs exist; use all the guidance and help they can offer.

> **Case Study 2**: You dutifully obtain a peer evaluation and student evaluations for your first ever college class. The peer evaluator is fairly positive, but the student evaluations are scathing.

It is not at all unusual for first-time instructors to collect less than stellar student evaluations. Do not despair! Novice instructors, sensitive instructors, anxious instructors (a very common three-way combination) could consider sitting with the fairly positive peer evaluator (presumably a more experienced instructor) and objectively sifting through the student numbers and comments. More seasoned instructors can help parse the ignorable comments ("has a face like a horse," "I hate math," "class starts too early") from the actionable ones ("didn't answer emails," "too much busywork," "talks too fast"). Think through and make revisions to the class policies and procedures with as positive an attitude as possible, using the peer evaluator for moral support. Instructors who thoughtfully revise their courses based on peer and student feedback are much more likely to be retained, no matter their initial student evaluation numbers and comments.

> **Case Study 3**: You begin the term newly pregnant, and by week 8 of the 15-week term you begin experiencing severe morning sickness.

This too shall pass. Even if you are not telling anyone else yet about your pregnancy, confer with the chair, who receives secrets like this on nearly a daily basis. Of course, employ the usual tricks recommended by obstetricians (crackers, wrist bands, mints, other straws to furtively grasp). But with severe symptoms, consider other possible work arounds: moving a face-to-face course to be synchronous virtual, asking for a substitute for a month or so, or judiciously using sick days.

Example Lecture Notes

Lecture Notes Version 1
Tuesday

    A. Definition: Reliability is the degree of consistency of a measure

    B. Primary types of reliability

        1. Internal consistency reliability is a measure of how consistently individuals respond across items of a questionnaire

        2. Example

        3. Test-retest reliability is a measure of how consistently individuals respond to a questionnaire across time

        4. Example

        5. Inter-rater reliability is a measure of how consistently different raters judge the same characteristic

        6. Example

    C. Statistics used to assess reliability

        1. Cronbach's alpha

        2. Correlation

        3. Cohen's kappa

Lecture Notes Version 2
Tuesday

   A. Class logistics

   B. Reliability: Introduction

      1. Definition (Slide 1)

      2. Examples in the literature (Slides 2, 3, 4)

   C. Types of reliability

      1. Internal consistency (Slide 5)

      2. Example (Slide 6)

      3. Test-retest reliability (Slide 7)

      4. Example (Slide 8)

      5. Inter-rater reliability (Slide 9)

      6. Example (Slide 10)

   D. Statistics used to assess reliability

      1. Cronbach's alpha (Slide 11)

      2. Correlation (Slide 12)

      3. Cohen's kappa (Slide 13)

Lecture Notes Version 3
Tuesday and Thursday 3/5 & 3/7

A. Class logistics

   1. Exam 1 in two weeks 3/21/24

   2. Paper 2 due this Thursday 3/7/24

   3. Paper 1 graded by Tuesday 3/12

B. Probability: warm-up

   1. "My friend is unreliable." What does that mean to you? Write down a few descriptor words in two minutes.

   2. Discussion of terms and tie to scientific meaning of reliability.

C. Reliability: Overview

   1. Definition of reliability (Slide 1)

   2. Preview types of reliability (Slide 2)

   3. Preview formulas to measure reliability (Slide 3)

   4. Personal story about reliability: Extremely agitated colleague accusing me of besmirching another colleague's character because word got out I was calculating Cohen's kappa on raters' scores

D. Internal consistency reliability

   1. Definition (Slide 4)

   2. Formula (Slide 5)

   3. Examples (Slide 6,7)

E. Test-retest reliability

   1. Definition (Slide 8)

   2. Formula (Slide 9)

   3. Examples (Slide 10,11)

F. Inter-rater reliability

   1. Definition (Slide 12)

   2. Formula (Slide 13)

   3. Examples (Slide 14,15)

G. Warm up

   1. "Your point is valid." What does that mean to you? Write down a few descriptor words in two minutes.

   2. Discussion of terms and tie to scientific meaning of validity

H. Validity: Overview

   1. Definition of validity (Slide 16)

   2. Preview types of validity (Slide 17)

   3. Preview formulas to measure validity (Slide 18)

   4. Personal story about validity: The California Psychological Inventory is designed to measure personality characteristics in a non-obvious / non-face valid manner. Participants got mad when answering True/False to the item "I prefer a bath to a shower."

Compare and Contrast

- Amount of content. If teaching more than once per week, preparing the entire week's worth of content, slides, and activities gives more wiggle room, in the event that you move more quickly through the material than anticipated. The best lecture notes have an "emergency activity," to the same effect.

- Class logistics. Even with deadlines embedded in the learning management platform, even with electronic reminders via email, even with virtual announcements: your personal voice reminding students what they will be doing in the future (exams, papers) and what you will be doing in the future (grading) establishes rapport and community. Rather than assume you will remember to discuss class logistics or know the details off the top of your head, a thorough accounting prompts transmission of accurate details.

- Brevity. Let your slides do the heavy lifting of content. With the exception of very specific definitions or formulae, which are fine in slides, reading detailed, carefully worded statements, word for word, either in lecture notes or slides can spike boredom on the part of the student and anxiety on the part of the instructor.

- Interactive elements. The introduction of interactive elements, particularly in the beginning of class, takes students' eyes off the instructor and on to one another. Such activities also signal that students are not there to watch a show (often majorly anxiety-inducing for the instructor) but to learn (possibly minorly anxiety-inducing for the students).

- Examples. Providing examples, often several for more complex topics, adds interest and aids student learning. Particularly for anxious instructors, who may freeze up when trying to think of examples on the fly, inserting ideas for examples in the lecture notes is a good idea.

- Mix of content. Engaged and interested students serve as a wonderful cheering section for novice or anxious instructors. Interweaving student activities with lecture keeps students on their toes. Similarly, interweaving content can keep motivation higher. Rather than clump all discussion of formulae at the end, for example, pulling in each formula as needed may keep students attentive longer.

CHAPTER 11

New Instructor Checklist

Compensation

    Amount of pay per month

    First and last check date

    Benefits

    Parking

Professional Expectations

    Requirements for office hours, including location

    Requirements for attending meetings / retreats / social events / graduations

    Opportunities for professional development / travel

    Union?

    Policies for peer teaching evaluations

    Policies for student teaching evaluations

    Procedures for reporting sick leave

    Opportunities for teaching assistants / graders / peer mentors

Class Details
- Textbooks required / textbooks discouraged?
- Mandatory Student Learning Objectives?
- Mandatory assessments?

Classroom Details
- Location of department office
- Location of classroom, if appropriate
- Location of bathrooms
- Locations of stairways, in the event of an evacuation
- Keys to enter building? Classroom?

Grades
- Technology required for recording points
- Technology required for posting grades
- Due date for grades
- Policies for "incomplete"
- Policies for cheating
- Policies for plagiarism

Administrative Support
- Do I have a mailbox?
- Do I have an office?
- Where / how to make copies
- Where / how to access library

New Instructor Checklist

Troubleshooting

    Janitor service

    Building maintenance

    Technology support

Emergency procedures

    Police (differences between campus police and city police)

    Ambulance

    Fire

    Erratic student behavior

Chapter 12

Teaching Adventures Bingo Sheet

Class spontaneously applauds you	Student nominates you for an award	Student tattles on you to university president	Nervous diarrhea the night before first day of class	Student develops a crush on you
Student mutiny!	The fire alarm rings during class	Class insists on group hug	Student throws up in class	Dog throws up in class!
Student has a seizure	Your answer key is incorrect	WILD CARD!	Classroom equipment catches on fire	Class ends much too early
You drop the f-bomb in class	Student cries in class	Student parent complains to you	You fall down in class	Student passes out in class
You cry in class	No one finishes the exam	You hang up on your Zoom class	Student leaves drunken phone messages	Student shows up for class high

Index

academic freedom, 15–16
accessibility, 10–11
active learning activities, 24–28,

Bingo sheet, teaching adventures, 113
Bloom's taxonomy, 16–17, *18*
breaks, 52–53
burnout, 74–75

captain's hat, *51*, 59
cheating, 7, 37–38, 40–41, 47–48, 89–90
classroom management: angry class, 57–58; cigarette, *31*, 35; confused class, 83–84; distracted class, 54–55; ghosting class, 7, 58, 59; kind class, 59; lethargic class, 55, 56; mutinous class, 78-79; unruly class, 56, 57
course schedule: experiential-centered small courses, 8–9, 79, *79*; sequential topics courses, 8–9, 80, *80*; cumulative topics courses, 8–9, 80, *81*

examinations: closed-ended versus open-ended examination questions, 32–35, *32*; no-stakes versus low-stakes versus high-stakes examinations, 36–37; length of examination, 35–36; open-book versus closed-book examinations, 36; tightly timed versus loosely timed examinations, 36
emails, 3, 97–100
emergencies, 64
extra credit, 5

fox, *15*, 20

grades, 5

instructor evaluations: peer evaluations, 71; student evaluations, 71–72, 101, 102
instructor impairment: anxiety, 68–70, 75; physical or emotional illness, 73, 101, 102

learning management systems, 11–12

lecture notes, 20–22, 103–8
lotus, *67*, 75

new instructor checklist, 109–111

office hours, 3, 62–64

papers: iterative papers, 39–40; no-stakes versus low-stakes versus high-stakes papers, 40
presentations: individual student presentations, 41–42; group student presentations, 42–43
plagiarism, 7, 89–90

rubrics: simple rubrics, 43–44, 91–93; detailed rubrics, 45, 91–93

slides, 22–24, 85–87
student learning objectives, 5,
student names, 56, 96
syllabus: creating the syllabus, 2–14; changing the syllabus, 12–13, 77–78

textbooks, 4
trolls, *1*, 5,

Zoom, 19–20

About the Author

Constance Jones earned her BA in psychology from the University of California, Berkeley, and her PhD in human development and family studies from the Pennsylvania State University. She joined the faculty in the Department of Psychology at California State University, Fresno, in 1993. Constance (aka "Mama Jones" to her graduate students) served as chair of the department for almost 10 years, allowing her to add others' stories of teaching successes and mishaps to her own personal repertoire.

www.ingramcontent.com/pod-product-compliance
Lightning Source LLC
Chambersburg PA
CBHW030657230426
43665CB00011B/1135